BROTRS

THE WEEK LO

BROTHERS AND SISTERS:
Developmental, Dynamic, and Technical Aspects of the Sibling Relationship

edited by
Salman Akhtar, m.d.,
and Selma Kramer, m.d.

JASON ARONSON INC.
Northvale, New Jersey
London

This book was set in 12 pt. Garamond and printed and bound by Book-mart Press, Inc., of North Bergen, NJ.

10 9 8 7 6 5 4 3 2 1

Library of Congress Cataloging-in-Publication Data

Brothers and sisters : developmental, dynamic, and technical aspects
   of the sibling relationship / edited by Salman Akhtar and Selma
   Kramer.
        p. cm.
   Includes bibliographical references and index.
   ISBN 0-7657-0203-7 (alk. paper)
   1. Brothers and sisters. 2. Sibling rivalry. I. Akhtar, Salman,
1946 July 31– II. Kramer, Selma.
   BF723.S43B78   1999
   306.875—dc21   98–54403

Printed in the United States of America on acid-free paper. For information and catalog write to Jason Aronson Inc., 230 Livingston Street, Northvale, NJ 07647-1726. Or visit our website: www.aronson.com

To the memory

of Margaret S. Mahler

teacher, friend, source of inspiration

Contents

Acknowledgment

The chapters in this book, with the exception of the last one, were originally presented as papers at the 29th Annual Margaret S. Mahler Symposium on Child Development held on May 2, 1998, in Philadelphia. First and foremost, therefore, we wish to express our gratitude to the Margaret S. Mahler Psychiatric Research Foundation. We are also grateful to Stephen L. Schwartz, M.D., Acting Chairman of the Department of Psychiatry and Human Behavior, Jefferson Medical College, as well as to the Philadelphia Psychoanalytic Institute and Society for their shared sponsorship of the symposium. Many colleagues from the Institute and Society helped during the symposium, and we remain grateful to them. Finally we wish to acknowledge our sincere appreciation of Maryann Nevin for her efficient organization of and assistance during the symposium, and her outstanding skills in the preparation of this book's manuscript.

Contributors

Ricardo Ainslie, Ph.D.
Professor and Director, Counseling Psychology, University of
Texas at Austin; Doctoral Training Program, University of
Texas at Austin; Faculty, Houston-Galveston Psychoanalytic
Institute

Salman Akhtar, M.D.
Professor of Psychiatry, Jefferson Medical College; Training and
Supervising Analyst, Philadelphia Psychoanalytic Institute

Rosemary Balsam, M.D.
Associate Clinical Professor of Psychiatry, Yale School of Medi-
cine; Training and Supervising Analyst, Western New England
Institute for Psychoanalysis

Harold P. Blum, M.D.
Clinical Professor of Psychiatry, New York University School
of Medicine; Training and Supervising Analyst, The Psychoana-

lytic Association of New York; Executive Director, Sigmund Freud Archives

Selma Kramer, M.D.
Professor of Psychiatry, Jefferson Medical College; Training and Supervising Analyst, Philadelphia Psychoanalytic Institute

Henri Parens, M.D.
Professor of Psychiatry, Jefferson Medical College; Training and Supervising Analyst, Philadelphia Psychoanalytic Institute

Robert C. Prall, M.D.
Child, Adolescent and Adult Psychoanalyst; Visiting Professor of Child Psychiatry, Medical College of Pennsylvania

Barbara Shapiro, M.D.
Associate Professor of Pediatrics, University of Pennsylvania School of Medicine; Faculty, Philadelphia Psychoanalytic Institute

Vamık D. Volkan, M.D.
Professor of Psychiatry and Director of the Center for the Study of Mind and Human Interaction, University of Virginia; Training and Supervising Analyst, Washington Psychoanalytic Institute

1

BEYOND THE PARENTAL ORBIT: BROTHERS, SISTERS, AND OTHERS

Salman Akhtar, M.D.,
and Selma Kramer, M.D.

Psychoanalytic theory of personality development seems to have evolved in four incremental phases. In the pioneering *first* phase, discoveries of the instinctual substrate of human motivations, childhood seduction and, later, of the Oedipus complex were made. The child's burgeoning ego capacities and his or her interactions with the father were focused on as the central structure building elements (e.g., Abraham 1927, Fenichel 1945, Freud 1905, 1915, 1923, Hartmann 1939). In the *second* phase, clinical and heuristic attention shifted to the preoedipal development. Various object-relations, developmental, and self-oriented theoretical perspectives (e.g., Fairbairn 1952, A. Freud 1965, Kernberg 1975, 1976, Klein 1946, 1952, 1957, Kohut 1971, 1977, Mahler et al. 1975, Winnicott 1965) appeared on the scene. Actual observation of parent–child interactions began. Focus of study and theory building gradually shifted toward the mother. In the *third* phase, a methodologically sound renewed interest in the father's role emerged. Investigators began to address his role not only in the superego formation but also in the separation-individuation phase and in the structurally reorganizing turbulence of adolescence (Abelin 1971, Blos 1985, Cath et al. 1982, Ross 1979, 1982). Finally, in the current, *fourth* phase, a growing interest in moving beyond the parental objects is discernible.[1] Analysts are beginning to investigate the role of grandparents and siblings in the growth and development of a child's personality (Ainslie 1985, Balsam 1988, Cath et al. 1982, Colonna and Newman 1983, Neubauer 1983, Solnit 1983, Volkan and Ast 1997).[2]

Representing this contemporary trend, we focus here on the sibling relationship and provide an overview of the factors that shape the nature of this experience. In doing so, we automatically acknowledge that a child's relationship with his or her sibling(s) includes a wide range of experiences. Just the way not having any siblings at all prevents the child from being displaced but also leaves him lonely, having siblings has its own pros and cons. On the positive side, it offers the child an opportunity to share, cooperate, elaborate fantasy, borrow psychic strength, and socialize beyond the parental orbit (Provence and Solnit 1983). On the negative side, the relationship provides a fertile soil for envy, jealousy, unhealthy rivalry, resentment, and even hatred.[3]

---

[1]While the importance of relatives other than parents is being recognized, the attention paid to the role of animals and inanimate objects in child development, with the exception of the contributions of Frosch (1966), Searles (1960), and Akhtar and Volkan (in press), still remains inoptimal.

[2]The citations of literature here are hardly exhaustive. Only very select, pioneering contributions are mentioned in order to underscore the trends being discussed.

[3]Neubauer (1983) provides succinct definitions of "rivalry," "envy," and "jealousy" in this regard. "*Rivalry* is the competition among siblings for the exclusive or preferred care from the person they share. . . . *Envy* refers to the wish for the possession of attributes that a parent or sibling has, such as penis, strength, breasts. . . . *Jealousy* is the competition with a sibling or parent for the love of the person whom they share" (pp. 326–327, author's italics).

While the economy of libido and aggression in this relational matrix is often shifting, it is not infrequent to find the overall balance tilting in one or the other direction. As a result, some such relationships are experienced as "good" and others "bad." More often, ambivalence prevails and the relationship continues to evolve throughout childhood, adolescence, and even during adult life. Moreover, its nature and intensity seem to be governed by a large number of factors which we will attempt to illustrate by a survey of the pertinent literature as well as by some brief clinical vignettes.[4]

FACTORS AFFECTING THE SIBLING RELATIONSHIP

Parental Availability

An important factor governing the nature of the relationship between siblings is whether their parents are alive or dead. If parental deaths occur very early and the siblings are adopted and raised in separate foster homes, little relationship might exist between them. On the other hand, one particular child might harbor unconscious fantasies of the other sibling being somehow responsible for the parental deaths (Shambaugh 1961). In that case, a deep and sustained, albeit hateful, internal bond might develop between them. More often, the absence of parents intensifies the sibling relationship in positive ways.[5] This is the only abiding bond now available. In such circumstances, the sibling relationship must be protected.

---

[4]The clinical material cited here is brief and disguised, hence not suitable for borrowing for research purposes. Vignettes 1, 2, 4 and 5 come from Selma Kramer's and vignettes 3 and 6 from Salman Akhtar's clinical work.

[5]The soothing availability of a sibling is often strikingly helpful in situations of a partial loss of a parent, such as following divorce. Children with siblings usually adjust better to divorce than do only children (Etezady 1983, Wallerstein and Kelly 1980).

Siblings left alone, as in war, natural catastrophe, or abandonment by parents, are often in high risk situations since the sibling relationship is the most that is left for such children, even though it is not adequate by comparison to have a permanent adult caretaker. In these instances, the sibling relationship is burdened with and challenged by tasks that belong to the dynamics of a child/adult relationship. [Solnit 1983, p. 283]

Significantly, in situations where parents are alive and living together, adult siblings maintain an invisible connection with each other through the parental presence. Visits to the parental home, not infrequently on holidays involving large and sumptuous meals, provide them an opportunity for receiving emotional refueling not only from parents but from each other as well. This was evident in a comment made by a middle-aged colleague following her only remaining parent's death. She said that it felt like a trunk of a huge tree has been uprooted and now she and her siblings are like unconnected branches of that tree, and that "from now on, we will have to make an extra effort to stay connected."

Relationship between Parents

The nature of the sibling relationship is also affected by how good or bad the relationship is between their parents. When love and mutual respect exist between the two parents, children have an opportunity to observe instances of their sharing libidinal supplies offered by life and tolerating the aggression emanating from divergent opinions. Feeling affectionately held and erotically satisfied, the spouses have little leftover aggression to be directed toward children. In keeping with the colloquial assertion that the rich get richer and the poor get poorer, a loving relationship between parents tends to generate a positive tie between the siblings, and a troubled relationship between parents adversely affects the sibling bond. In situations of marital discord, especially if it is characterized by venomous attacks and violence between the spouses, aggression readily spills over onto the children and compromises their ego capacities to retain a loving relationship with each other.

Parental Behavior toward Children

The relationship between siblings is also affected by how their parents behave toward them. Parents may promote positive feelings and relationships or may foster difficulties between siblings.

> It is nearly universal for parents initially to harbor an idealized image of the future of the firstborn and later, when the second child is expected, of their children's future relationship with each other. This idealization is in conflict with a fear of the impending competitive demands of the children on them. Even under the best conditions, such an idealized fantasy must meet with disappointment. [Kris and Ritvo 1983, p. 312]

How parents handle this disappointment is crucial. If there is psychopathology within or between the parents, the requisite mourning does not take place. Splitting occurs and idealization is maintained toward one child. The resulting favoritism harms the other child. The rejection felt by the latter is compounded by the not infrequent overt mistreatment of him or her that accompanies such favoritism. Together the two factors poison the sibling relationship, often in lasting ways.[6] To wit, a situation of this sort prevailed in the life of Margaret Mahler, to whom this book is dedicated. Mahler was born, unwanted, nine months and one week after her parents' marriage. Her mother had very little to do with her, even during the first year of her life. Margaret grew up feeling "full of frustrated rage at

---

[6]Patients' jealousy of their therapist's other patients, while multiply determined, often emanates from such historical background.

the rejecting mother whom [she] loved nevertheless" (Mahler, in Stepansky 1988, p. 4). The situation worsened for her upon the birth of a sibling.

> The arrival of my sister, Suzanne, four years after my birth only aggravated my sense of maternal rejection. She was very much a "wanted" child, and she awakened our mother's maternal instincts—instincts that, for me, had lain dormant. For my sister, my mother got up at night; she accepted and loved the younger child in a way she never accepted and loved me. . . . My mother's continual demonstrations of affection and solicitousness in my presence only fueled my sense of victimization: I was angry at my mother and full of contempt for the sister who, as I saw it, had it all too easy. [Mahler, in Stepansky 1988, pp. 4–5]

The hostility between Margaret and her sister Suzanne lasted until the latter's death. This is a testimony to the profound impact of grossly preferential treatment by parents of one child over the other upon the relationship between siblings. In the case of Margaret Mahler and her sister, the difference in maternal attitude seems to have emanated from the timing of their births and the "wanted" and "unwanted" nature of the two maternal pregnancies.

At times, more subtle factors are at work in determining how a parent responds to a particular child and how that attitude affects the relationship of that child with his or her siblings. One such instance involves parents who are grieving over the death of a child. Often such parents deposit the representation of the deceased into a "replacement" child (Cain and Cain 1964, Poznanski 1972, Volkan and Ast 1997) conceived soon after the older sibling's death. The grieving parents then influence the newly arrived child to assimilate this object representation into his or her self representation and thus keep the dead child "alive." The resulting split in the psyche contributes to various pathological outcomes (Volkan 1987) and a life torn by the dual agenda of living out the imagined destiny of a dead sibling alongside that of one's own authentic self.

Social Siblings

The term *social siblings* (Colonna and Newman 1983, p. 303) is used to denote biologically unrelated children living together and being raised as brothers and sisters. Israeli kibbutz children and adopted children in general constitute two prominent examples of social siblings.[7] The relationship between them differs in important ways from that between actual biological children of the same parents. This is most evident in instances where one of the children in the family is adopted. Despite best efforts, parents frequently falter in being able to give equal amounts and quality of attention to their biological and adopted offspring (Jacobs 1988). Their biological offspring often hold a place of importance in their heart that cannot be rivaled by their adopted children. While immensely gratifying to the biological child, such privilege also results in guilt. The wish, on the part of both the biological and the adopted sibling, that the latter be returned to his family of origin also induces guilt in the face of the love being offered by parents. Such internal turmoil can have a deleterious impact on the relationship between the siblings. Moreover, a child's learning about the adoption of a sibling stirs up an uncertainty in his mind "not only about the circumstances of that sibling's birth, but about his own origin

---

[7]Psychoanalytic candidates in analysis with the same training analyst constitute a special variety of social siblings. Depending on a multitude of factors, their relationship with each other can either be riddled with jealousy and competitiveness or imbued with a sense of fraternity; often the sentiments between them are mixed and may need long-term working through. Many striking examples of the failure of such working through can be found among the pioneers of psychoanalysis, especially the analysands of Freud, who often undermined each other in order to gain the master's approval long after their analyses with him were over.

as well" (Jacobs 1988, p. 33). The psychological impact of adoption on the siblings of adopted children is thus profound and might complicate not only their own intrapsychic lives but their relationship with their siblings as well.

Twins and Twinning

The relationship between twins and that between non-twin siblings seems to differ in important ways. Both biological and environmental factors contribute to this difference. Monozygotic twins share more genetic material with each other than do ordinary siblings and therefore start their psychic lives with closely allied temperaments, providing a fundamental template of mutual empathy that can, at times, be of uncanny proportions (Engel 1975). Their biological affinity can be heightened or compromised by the manner of their upbringing. In this context, the actual behavior of the parents toward the twins as well as the more subtle communications of the parental unconscious fantasies is important (Ainslie 1985, Volkan and Ast 1997). Giving the two children similar-sounding names, dressing them in matching outfits, referring to them as "the twins," and frequently mistaking one child for the other are among the parental behaviors that contribute to the blurring of the intrapsychic boundaries between them. In contrast is the parental tendency to emphasize their differences. This often arises from a healthy regard for the autonomous existence of the two siblings. However, in situations of anxiety and especially when there is a tendency toward intrapsychic splitting within the parents' own minds, such underlining of differences can become caricatured and even pathological. One twin then is labeled "the good one" and the other "the bad one."

Case 1

> A 10-year-old, good-looking girl who was one of a pair of nonidentical twins was brought to me because of her poor

school performance. She possessed above-average intelligence and yet was constantly lagging behind in her studies. From birth on, she had been labeled the "dumber but prettier" twin. Much less was expected of her by her parents, an attitude imperceptibly picked up and enacted by her teachers from kindergarten onward. One of her teachers even said to me that this girl "does not have to *do*, she merely has to *be*." The child, it seems, had missed both the gratifications and the ego-enhancing frustrations entailed in studying. Somewhere along the way she had internalized the lack of expectations imposed upon her by her parents.

Strikingly different treatment of twins by their parents results in a strain on the relationship between the siblings. The relationship between twins is both gifted with extraordinary assets (e.g., empathy, narcissistic mirroring) and cursed with undue psychic burdens (e.g., intensified need for self definition, lifelong effort to reclaim that half of one's identity that had been relegated to the other twin during the formative years). The deep affinity and the comparably intense hostility that can exist between twins has been traced by authors citing the examples of biblical figures such as Cain and Abel (Grinberg 1963), and eminent literary writers such as Anthony and Peter Shaffer (Kiell 1983).

Before leaving the topic of twins, we should note the phenomenon of "psychological twinning" (Ainslie 1985, Joseph and Tabor 1961, Meyers 1996, Volkan and Ast 1997). Describing such pairing of two siblings, Volkan and Ast (1997) note that

> biological twinship is not a necessary condition for twinning. The pair, however speak of themselves as "twins" or "blood siblings." Sometimes they have ritually bonded themselves together by pricking their fingers and mixing their blood. . . . [T]hey exhibit a need for daily physical contact and closeness and they may engage in mutual masturbation. They usually share daydreams in which both

are "actors" or "actresses" involved in joined adventures
which result in their remaining a pair forever. [p. 106]

Such intermingling of identity occurs more often between
children who are less than two years apart in age (Shopper 1974)
and also more often between a sister and a brother than between
same-sex siblings (Volkan and Ast 1997). In any case, closeness
of such proportions usually comes to a crashing halt when the
older of the two siblings reaches adolescence. A greater psychological separation between the two then begins, but the memory
of their twinning remains for a long time, if not forever. This
psychic residue might then function as a transitional fantasy, a
psychic space of solace to which one can retreat in moments of
loneliness, narcissistic defeat, or anguish. Or it might become a
structural substrate needing constant repudiation in an individual sibling's search for authenticity. While seen in "psychological twins," this search is perhaps more common in actual,
biological twins.

Case 2

A young woman sought help in separating psychologically
from her identical twin. She said that she had always felt a
strong need to establish an independent identity. At the
same time, she was afraid that she could not survive without her sister. Inquiry about her childhood background revealed that she and her sister were always called "the twins"
rather than by their individual names. Often one was ad-
dressed by the other's name, a mistake facilitated by the
fact that they looked so much alike. Neither twin dated
until they were well into college years. Soon after gradua-
tion, my patient's twin sister got married. My patient felt
depressed and abandoned. She felt that her only path to
strength was to move to Philadelphia, a city far away from
where her sister lived. Not surprisingly, the move was not
psychologically successful. My patient felt increasing anxi-

ety and began having troublesome dreams in which she was not bodily intact. Unfortunately, she could not allow herself to remain in treatment long enough since she started to experience the dread that she could become as deeply attached to me as she had been to her sister.

The rapprochement subphase-like ambitendency, the desperate striving for autonomy, and the deep-seated dread of merger manifested by this patient are reminiscent of the protagonist of Judith Rossner's (1977) successful novel *Attachments*.

Sex of the Siblings

Having an opposite-sex sibling brings different challenges to a growing child's ego than having a same-sex sibling. It may deprive the two children of sharing certain play activities and real and/or fantasized adventures. By providing a greater exposure to the opposite-sex genitals, it might also increase penis envy and castration anxiety.

Case 3

> A young mother with a 7-year-old son and a 5-year-old daughter reported an intriguing behavior on the part of her daughter. Fond of a family friend of theirs, the little girl initiated a game that she labeled as "blind animals" with him. This family friend would draw the picture of an animal (e.g., elephant, turtle, owl) and she would gleefully scribble out the animal's eyes, bursting into laughter and saying that "this animal is blind."
>
> When her mother asked me why the girl did this, I suggested that perhaps she was seeing something that she did not want to see. Dialogue along these lines led to my learning that while the girl was not witnessing the primal scene, she was indeed exposed to something that could be anxiety producing. The mother bathed the two children to-

gether in the tub every day, exposing the little girl to her older brother's genitals. As we discussed its potential impact on the little girl, the mother put an end to this practice. The little girl soon lost interest in playing the "blind animals" game with the family friend!

The opposite-sex sibling situation can also become a fertile ground for the displacement of psychosexual fantasies originally directed toward parents. The expectable erotic interest between siblings then becomes intensified and potential for acting out the oedipal fantasies is increased.

Case 4

A little girl was brought to me for the treatment of a severe eating problem. As we worked together, a history of sexual abuse by a sibling gradually emerged. I learned that her parents often left her in the care of her seven-years-older brother with no adult supervision at all. She had been forced by this brother to perform fellatio on him. The brother was born soon after his father left to serve in the second World War and had not seen his father until he returned from the service. The brother felt that the father was an interloper who had taken his place in sleeping with the mother. The father was eager for another child and soon impregnated the mother. Upon the arrival of the new child, my patient, the father treated her with much tenderness and warmth. This fueled the brother's sense of rivalry with his sister.

Both parents had difficulty believing me (indeed, they were shocked) when I suggested that their little daughter's feeding problem had something to do with the "baby-sitting arrangements." They refused to follow up on my suggestion that their son also needed treatment. Their daughter, they said, warranted treatment because she was good.

The father felt very angry with his son and did not want him to have the benefit of analysis!

The patient improved considerably with treatment. A follow-up visit years later brought forth further interesting material. I learned that the brother had been disowned by the parents. He later succumbed to a chronic illness during which he was visited only by my patient. Talking about all this, she felt quite angry with me, feeling that it was my fault that her parents had treated her brother so badly. I pointed out that the information about his having sexually abused her in childhood was derived from her own associations. She refused to believe me and stormed out of my office.

To my great surprise, she asked for another appointment a week later. Upon arrival, she appeared quite contrite and revealed a dream that she had had the night after our previous session. The dream went as follows: "I was sucking something, maybe a big toe. It became bigger and bigger. Then something popped and white fluid spurted out." With tears in her eyes and a knowing look on her face, she added, "I must have been wrong when I told you that you were wrong about what happened between me and my brother."

Parallel to such problematic occurrences, the scenario of opposite-sex siblings might also offer certain psychosocial advantages. The availability of an object toward whom erotic impulses originally directed at the parents can be diverted might facilitate the resolution of the Oedipus complex. It is as if the child with an opposite-sex sibling gets a second chance to work through and renounce such prohibited strivings.[8] At the same

---

[8]Ancient Hindu belief compares a man's having grown up with sisters to having been born and raised in a town with a river. Both experiences are felt to give a certain restraint, gratitude, and humility to the individual's character.

time, it should be noted that erotic interest in siblings might also arise independently and not entirely be a displacement of love of the parental figures. In either case, unresolved unconscious attachment to opposite-sex siblings, especially if they are older, can underlie the choice of love partners in adult life (Abend 1984).

Age Difference

There is no ideal time gap between the birth of siblings since each developmental phase has its own psychological hazards that can be intensified by the arrival of another child. However, it does seem that the birth of a sibling during the rapprochement subphase (from about 16 to about 24 months) of separation-individuation (Mahler et al. 1975) greatly complicates the older sibling's preoedipal development (see also Greenacre 1950 in this regard). Additionally, if a second child is born when the first one is already 5 to 6 years old, the latter might respond with intense resentment, since he or she has by then become used to being an only child. Such hateful rivalry of an older child toward his younger sibling received much attention from Freud (1917), who stated that

> a child who has been put into second place by the birth of a brother or sister, and who is now for the first time almost isolated from his mother, does not easily forgive her this loss of place; feelings which in an adult would be described as greatly embittered arise in him and are often the basis of a permanent estrangement. [p. 334]

Freud (1900, 1910, 1917) also cited many examples of older siblings hating younger ones and said that many people "who loved their brothers and sisters and would feel bereaved if they were to die, harbour evil wishes against them in their unconscious, dating from earlier times; and these are capable of being realized in dreams" (1910, p. 251).

In families with more than four or five children, one or the other child often gets exposed to such traumas.[9] They become even more pathogenic if feeling displaced by younger siblings is coupled with neglect or abuse from parents. Resentment toward the younger sibling then builds up and might lead to abusive behavior, at times even death wishes (Freud 1900, 1910) toward him or her.[10]

Case 5

Michael was brought for analysis when he was 9 years of age. The eldest of five children (two boys and three girls), he stuttered, did poorly in school, and fought constantly with his younger brother. History revealed that Michael was physically abused by his father and had many fears. Prominent among them was his dread of having additional siblings born, a dread that only thinly veiled his deep hostility toward his younger siblings. He once said, "Our family is like the Chinese. No matter how many you kill, there are more and more born!"

   To complicate matters, I became pregnant with my second child in the course of Michael's analysis. He had many sadistic fantasies and was frightened by them. He fantasized that instead of being delivered "down" the baby would be

---

[9]Explicating this very dynamic, I have elsewhere (Akhtar 1990) suggested that "the genetic determinant of having been a dearly loved first child whose mother gave birth to six other children by the time he was merely 10 years old might have predisposed Freud to a certain wistful, chronic inner aloneness" (p. 385) which, coupled with other factors, contributed to his constant feeling of not receiving adequate attention.

[10]Actual death of a younger sibling can therefore result in profound, lifelong guilt. At the same time, there can be a surprising blockage of memories from early childhood, indicating the existence of frozen grief. Such loss can also fuel artistic and literary creativity (Pollock 1970). The varying impact of early sibling loss in the lives of Freud and Guntrip has been elucidated by Rudnytsky (1988), and Fanos (1996) provides an up-to-date survey of literature on sibling loss.

delivered "up," rupturing my uterus and causing the baby and me to bleed to death.

On a finer level than mere calendar months lies the issue of "developmental distance" (Solnit 1983, p. 283) that exists between two siblings. This refers to the ego resilience and skill vis-à-vis levels of excitation and frustration as well as the ego capacities for regulation, anticipation, planning, and adaptation.

> When siblings are separated by more developmental space, they may be living in widely separated developmental epochs (e.g., a 2 year old and his 9 year old sibling). Such siblings may still have a closer community of interests than either of them has with an adult, but their ease in communicating, empathizing, and identifying with each other is not nearly as great as in siblings who are developmentally close to each other. [p. 284]

Before leaving this section, we should note the situation of the abused younger sibling. Faced with such constant devaluation, he or she might internalize these hostile dictates and begin masochistically devaluing him- or herself.[11]

A Sibling with a Special Status

Finally, the relationship between two siblings is altered if one of them is somehow "special." This "specialness" can emanate from either positive or negative factors. Included among the former are extraordinary talents and beauty, which often cause the parents to idealize that particular child, leading to the intensification of envy and rivalry in his or her siblings. Included among the latter are congenital defects and chronic illness in a

---

[11]The popular Persian saying "Sag baash, biraader-e-Khurd na bash" (literally: "it is better to be a dog than to be a younger brother") gives a crystal-clear vision of such agony.

child that draw the parental attention away from healthier siblings. A handicapped or sickly child not only requires extra care from parents themselves but often mobilizes the parents to enlist the help of the healthy sibling to show special consideration toward him or her (Bergmann and Wolfe 1971). The healthy child is made to take on undue responsibilities and adopt ego attitudes beyond his or her developmental level. The dependency needs of the healthy child are thus cast aside, leading to the development of a pseudo-independent, unduly self-reliant "false self" (Winnicott 1965) that hides the thwarted needy self. Hatred toward the sick or handicapped sibling and guilt emanating from such hatred also continue to exist on an unconscious level, often distorting the life's course in peculiar ways.

Case 6

> While setting up an appointment via telephone, a patient asked me twice whether my office building had a name, such as the Pan Am Building, the Chrysler Building, and so on. I was intrigued by his insistence, since I had already given him the street number of my building. I also made a mental note of the fact that both the buildings he mentioned were in New York and not in Philadelphia, where I practice. I politely repeated that my building did not have a name, keeping my sense of curiosity for later.
>
> The patient arrived for his first evaluative session promptly. He related a repeated pattern of failed business ventures and unsuccessful romantic relationships. Further inquiry, however, revealed that he inadvertently spoiled his chances in both realms, especially when success was just around the corner. This hinted toward the existence of anxiety and unconscious guilt.
>
> As I began to obtain some family history, I was surprised to find that he had an older brother. My surprise

came from the fact that the patient had a "junior" after his name. I was puzzled as to why, despite having an older brother, it was he who was named after his father. Upon my inquiring about it, he agreed that this was not customary but said that he had never thought about the reasons for this unusual situation. Further questioning revealed that his older brother was mildly mentally retarded. At this point, I ventured a hypothesis. Could it be that his older brother had at first been named after their father, only to be given a different name after the discovery of his retardation? The patient was moved by this suggestion and, though he did not remember hearing any such thing while growing up, began talking about his sadness about his brother and his guilt over his own achievements. I commented that it was therefore not surprising that he had attempted to undermine his success on many occasions. As all this came out, I became aware that he had unconsciously given me a clue to his problem by insisting that my building (me) have a bigger, better name than merely a number. Now I brought up our telephone conversation, thus attempting to demonstrate the workings of the unconscious and his readiness for a sibling transference.

CONCLUDING REMARKS

In a helicopter tour of the territory, we have offered a broad perspective on the variable nature and intensity of the sibling relationship. Among the factors that significantly impact upon this relationship are (1) the availability of parents, (2) the relationship between parents, (3) parental behavior toward their children, (4) biological versus social status of the sibling bond, (5) twin versus non-twin situations, (6) same-sex versus opposite-sex siblings, (7) age difference between siblings, and (8) special status (such as illness, handicap, or outstanding talent) of one of the siblings. In reviewing these factors, we have cited pertinent literature, illustrated some points by mentioning the lives of some pioneering figures in our profession, and offered brief clinical vignettes. While we have not discussed issues of psychoanalytic process and technique, our clinical material does demonstrate that seemingly oedipal transferences can actually emanate from sibling triangles (Sharpe and Rosenblatt 1994), that childhood abuse by siblings often enters the treatment in dramatic ways, and that many patients desperately try to establish a "twinship transference" (Kohut 1971) with the analyst, though not entirely without concurrent recoil from merger anxieties. These, and other themes that we have merely touched upon, are elaborated on in this book by distinguished adult and child psychoanalysts with a special interest in the sibling relationship. Together they offer a more comprehensive survey of the scattered literature on this topic, new insights regarding the multifaceted nature of the sibling bond, and pithy observations regarding the normal and pathological residues of this relationship in the adult mind. It is our hope that the contributions of Drs. Ainslie, Balsam, and Volkan, and their respective discussions by Drs. Parens, Blum, and Shapiro, as well as the concluding commentary by Dr. Prall, will further elucidate the profound nature of the relationship between siblings and its vicissitudes in fantasy, emotion, transference, and, above all, lived life.

REFERENCES

Abelin, E. L. (1971). The role of the father in the separation-individuation process. In *Separation-Individuation: Essays in Honor of Margaret Mahler*, ed. J. B. McDevitt and C. F. Settlage, pp. 229–253. New York: International Universities Press.

Abend, S. (1984). Sibling love and object choice. *Psychoanalytic Quarterly* 38:425–430.

Abraham, K. (1927). *Selected Papers on Psycho-Analysis*. New York: Brunner/Mazel.

Ainslie, R. (1985). *The Psychology of Twinship*. Lincoln, NE: University of Nebraska Press.

Akhtar, S. (1990). A review of N. Kiell's *Freud Without Hindsight: Reviews of His Work 1893–1939*. *International Review of Psycho-Analysis* 17:381–386.

Akhtar, S., and Volkan, V. D. (in press). *The Mental Zoo*. Madison, CT: International Universities Press.

Balsam, R. (1988). On being good: the internalized sibling with examples from late adolescent analyses. *Psychoanalytic Inquiry* 8:66–87.

Bergmann, T., and Wolfe, S. (1971). Observations of the reactions of healthy children to their chronically ill siblings. *Bulletin of the Philadelphia Association of Psychoanalysis* 21:145–161.

Blos, P. (1985). *Son and Father: Before and Beyond the Oedipus Complex*. New York: Free Press.

Cain, A. C., and Cain, B. S. (1964). On replacing a child. *Journal of the American Academy of Child Psychiatry* 3:443–456.

Cath, S., Gurwitt, A. R., and Ross, J. M., eds. (1982). *Father and Child: Developmental and Clinical Perspectives*. Boston: Little, Brown.

Colonna, A. B., and Newman, L. M. (1983). The psychoanalytic literature on siblings. *Psychoanalytic Study of the Child* 38:285–309. New Haven, CT: Yale University Press.

Engel, G. L. (1975). The death of a twin. *International Journal of Psycho-Analysis* 56:23–40.

Etezady, M. H. (1983). Panel report: psychoanalytic inferences concerning children of divorced parents. *Journal of the American Psychoanalytic Association* 31:247–258.

Fairbairn, W. R. D. (1952). *Psychoanalytic Studies of the Personality*. London: Tavistock.

Fanos, J. H. (1996). *Sibling Loss*. Hillsdale, NJ: Lawrence Erlbaum.

Fenichel, O. (1945). *The Psychoanalytic Theory of Neurosis*. New York: Norton.

Freud, A. (1965). *Normality and Pathology in Childhood: Assessments of Development. The Writings, Vol. 6*. New York: International Universities Press.

Freud, S. (1900). The interpretation of dreams. *Standard Edition* 4–5:1–622.

——— (1905). Three essays on the theory of sexuality. *Standard Edition* 7:123–244.

——— (1910). Leonardo daVinci—In memory of his childhood. *Standard Edition* 11:59–137.

——— (1915). Instincts and their vicissitudes. *Standard Edition* 14:111–140.

——— (1917). A childhood memory from "Dichtung und Wahrheit." *Standard Edition* 17:145–156.

——— (1923). The ego and the id. *Standard Edition* 19:3–66.

Frosch, J. (1966). A note on reality constancy. In *Psychoanalysis—A General Psychology*, ed. R. M. Loewenstein et al., pp. 349–376. New York: International Universities Press.

Greenacre, P. (1950). Special problems of early female sexual development. *Psychoanalytic Study of the Child* 5:122–138. New York: International Universities Press.

Grinberg, L. (1963). Rivalry and envy between Joseph and his brothers. *Samiksa* 17:130–171.

Hartmann, H. (1939). *Ego Psychology and the Problems of Adaptation*. New York: International Universities Press.

Jacobs, T. (1988). On having an adopted sibling: some psychoanalytic observations. *International Review of Psycho-Analysis* 15:25–35.

Joseph, E., and Tabor, J. (1961). The simultaneous analysis of a pair of identical twins and the twinning reaction. *Psychoanalytic Study of the Child* 16:275–299. New York: International Universities Press.

Kernberg, O. (1975). *Borderline Conditions and Pathological Narcissism*. New York: Jason Aronson.

—— (1976). *Object Relations Theory and Clinical Psychoanalysis*. New York: Jason Aronson.

Kiell, N. (1983). *Blood Brothers*. New York: International Universities Press.

Klein, M. (1946). Notes on some schizoid mechanisms. In *Envy and Gratitude and Other Works 1946–63*, pp. 1–24. New York: Free Press, 1975.

—— (1952). The mutual influences of the development of ego and id. In *Envy and Gratitude and Other Works 1946–63*, pp. 55–60. New York: Free Press, 1975.

—— (1957). Envy and gratitude. In *Envy and Gratitude and Other Works 1946–63*, pp. 176–235. New York: Free Press, 1975.

Kohut, H. (1971). *The Analysis of the Self*. New York: International Universities Press.

—— (1977). *Restoration of the Self*. New York: International Universities Press.

Kris, M., and Ritvo, S. (1983). Parents and siblings: their mutual influences. *Psychoanalytic Study of the Child* 38:311–324. New Haven, CT: Yale University Press.

Mahler, M. S., Pine, F., and Bergman, A. (1975). *The Psychological Birth of the Human Infant*. New York: Basic Books.

Meyers, H. (1996). Insufficient individuation and the reparative fantasy of twinship. In *Intimacy and Infidelity: Separation-Individuation Perspectives*, ed. S. Akhtar and S. Kramer, pp. 91–105. Northvale, NJ: Jason Aronson.

Neubauer, P. B. (1983). The importance of the sibling experience. *Psychoanalytic Study of the Child* 38:325–336. New Haven, CT: Yale University Press.

Pollock, G. H. (1970). Anniversary reactions, trauma, and mourning. *Psychoanalytic Quarterly* 39:347–371.

Poznanski, E. O. (1972). The "replacement child": a saga of unresolved parental grief. *Behavioral Pediatrics* 81:1190–1193.

Provence, S., and Solnit, A. J. (1983). Development-promoting aspects of the sibling experience: vicarious mastery. *Psychoanalytic Study of the Child* 38:337–351. New Haven, CT: Yale University Press.

Ross, J. M. (1979). Fathering: a review of some psychoanalytic contributions on paternity. *International Journal of Psycho-Analysis* 60:317–327.

—— (1982). Oedipus revisited: Laius and the "Laius complex." *Psychoanalytic Study of the Child* 37:169–187. New Haven, CT: Yale University Press.

Rossner, J. (1977). *Attachments*. New York: Simon & Schuster.

Rudnytsky, P. L. (1988). Redefining the revenant: guilt and sibling loss in Guntrip and Freud. *Psychoanalytic Study of the Child* 43:423–432. New Haven, CT: Yale University Press.

Searles, H. F. (1960). *The Non-human Environment in Normal Development and in Schizophrenia*. New York: International Universities Press.

Shambaugh, B. (1961). A study of loss reactions in a seven year old. *Psychoanalytic Study of the Child* 16:510–552. New York: International Universities Press.

Sharpe, S. A. and Rosenblatt, A. D. (1994). Oedipal sibling triangles. *Journal of the American Psychoanalytic Association* 42:491–523.

Shopper, M. (1974). Twinning reactions in nontwin siblings. *Journal of the American Academy of Child and Adolescent Psychiatry* 13:300–318.

Solnit, A. J. (1983). The sibling experience. *Psychoanalytic Study of the Child* 38:281–284. New Haven, CT: Yale University Press.

Stepansky, P. (1988). *The Memoirs of Margaret S. Mahler*. New York: Free Press.

Volkan, V. D. (1987). *Six Steps in the Treatment of Borderline Personality Organization*. Northvale, NJ: Jason Aronson.

Volkan, V. D., and Ast, G. (1997). *Siblings in the Unconscious and Psychopathology*. Madison, CT: International Universities Press.

Wallerstein, J. S., and Kelly, J. B. (1980). *Surviving the Breakup: How Children and Parents Cope with Divorce*. New York: Basic Books.

Winnicott, D. W. (1965). *The Maturational Processes and the Facilitating Environment*. Madison, CT: International Universities Press.

2

TWINSHIP AND TWINNING REACTIONS IN SIBLINGS

Ricardo Ainslie, Ph.D.

The theme of powerful sibling love, whether or not consummated, is, of course, extremely common in history, legend, and literature. Analysts have by and large regarded it, when it emerges in analytic work, as merely a preliminary layer, a less threatening derivative of the incestuous wishes and fantasies which involve the parents.

Abend 1984, p. 425

Over the course of the last decade a number of important psychoanalytic contributions have begun to shift the prior conventional wisdom regarding the place of sibling relationships in child development and in the psychodynamics that govern the emotional lives of adults. For example, the 1983 volume of the *Psychoanalytic Study of the Child* devoted considerable space to the multiple influences of siblings in development, including contributions from such leading theorists as Marianne Kris, Neubauer, Provence, Ritvo, and Solnit, among others. These contributions have been followed by others who have argued with increasing cogency that, while the importance of sibling rivalry and its consequences in mental life was an important early discovery of psychoanalysis, there is much more to be said about the role of siblings in development. Abend (1984), for example, described two analytic patients whose preference in love partners in adult life were "profoundly influenced by persistent unconscious attachments to older siblings" (p. 425). Importantly, Abend argued that these sibling attachments were not mere displacements for parental objects. In a 1988 contribution on siblings, Parens (1988) similarly notes that "sibling experiences of relationships are notably rich and tend to be more vital to development than is often suggested by the play we see of sibling transferences in the clinical situation" (p. 32). To be sure, analysts have always been attuned to such issues as sibling spacing, the impact of the birth of siblings, the impact of maternal pregnancy or miscarriage, and related issues. However, these considerations have often remained operationalized at the level of the "clinical arts" while a full conceptualization of the theoretical importance of sibling relations has lagged behind.

The emerging conceptualizations question the adequacy of our long-held convictions regarding the exclusive importance of parental objects in development, perspectives that all too often relegated siblings to a more ancillary role. Leichtman (1985), for example, has proposed that the presence of older siblings has a significant effect on a child's separation-individuation process and traces this impact as a parallel process to what transpires between child and parent. Similarly, Sharpe and Rosenblatt (1994) have recently argued

> that in families with multiple siblings, oedipal-like triangles develop among siblings and between siblings and parent that exhibit many of the characteristics of the Oedipal "parental" triangle. Such relationships are not solely displacements of parental Oedipal constellations, but may exist parallel to and relatively independent of the Oedipal "parental" triangle. Moreover, they often exert a definitive

> influence on the individual's later identifications, choice of
> adult love object, and patterns of object-relating [p. 492]

In sum, the proposition that siblings play a more substantive role in development than previously theorized is increasingly, if cautiously, explored in the psychoanalytic literature.

In the present contribution I explore the role of so-called twinning reactions in twin and non-twin siblings, tracing first the sources of the characteristic psychological features of twinning reactions within the twin situation. I then examine the concept as it applies to non-twin siblings. I conclude with a critique of the concept of twinning reactions, drawing from what we have learned about sibling and other close relationships in recent years.

TWINNING REACTIONS IN TWINS

The occurrence of twins is one domain within psychoanalytic theorizing where the profound impact of the sibling relationship has been unambiguously viewed as a defining developmental experience. In one of the more interesting and unusual accounts in the literature, Joseph and Tabor (1961) described their observations of the simultaneous analyses of a pair of adult identical twins. Aware of the unique opportunity that this circumstance afforded, the authors chose not to discuss their evolving analytic work with one another while reporting to a third analyst over the course of two years. A central feature of Joseph and Tabor's contribution was their identification of the *twinning reaction* as an important organizing dynamic in the psychology of these two patients. The twinning reaction, they suggested, "consists of: (1) mutual interidentification, and (2) part fusion of the self-representation and the object representation of the other member of the pair" (p. 277). Joseph and Tabor argued that these circumstances led to a diffuseness of ego boundaries between the twins.

The characteristic diffuse ego boundaries in twins activates a variety of strategies within the twinship to manage the anxieties produced by such states. One common strategy is to bifurcate identity characteristics into polarized traits such as male/female, active/passive, leader/follower, stronger/weaker smarter/less smart. Many theorists (e.g., Ablon et al. 1986, Arlow 1960, Athanassiou 1986, Joseph 1961, Prall 1990) have remarked on the tendency for twins to divide up the pool of available identity characteristics. Often, these polarized personality traits derive from differential identifications with mother and father, for example, or even from identifications with different aspects of the mother's personality. For example, one identical twin who occupied a feminine role in a masculine/feminine complementary relationship with his brother accounted for these traits this way. "My mother's maiden name is my middle name, and so I kind of think that I have a lot of traits from her. I have a lot of feminine traits from my mom, and I'm glad I have them [describes the fact that the two of them are very musically inclined]. [Twin brother] . . . he's sort of like dad . . . Dad did a lot of things that were 'macho' things, and he can see himself in [twin brother]."

Another significant motivation for the bifurcation of identity traits is to circumvent the powerful rivalrous, competitive feelings that permeate the twin relationship. To the extent that each twin is able to delineate a domain of selfhood, there is, at least potentially, a concomitant reduction in competitive feelings.

The polarization of identity characteristics, though quite commonplace among twins, often appears rather arbitrary, and, upon close inspection, lacks the fully metabolized (Kernberg 1976) quality that characterizes more mature object relationships as these become internalized into personality structure. Furthermore, the polarized identity characteristics are not necessarily stable, and they do not necessarily reflect actual talents or capacities. For example, in the case material presented by Joseph and Tabor, Twin B was regarded as the leader and he would protect the twins in fights. It thus came as a great surprise to twin A, the seemingly weaker, less masculine of the twins, when he outwrestled his twin brother and later defeated the twins' older brother in a fight. Evidence to the contrary notwithstanding, twin A felt that twin B was his superior in all aspects: appearance, strength, intelligence, and ability.

Similarly, in a set of twins I interviewed, one became the smart, intellectual twin within her family, while her sister became the athletic, less academically inclined twin (Ainslie 1997). Both twins subscribed to these descriptions of their characteristics, as did their family. In this way, the destabilizing stresses and anxieties that come from having a tenuous sense of self could be obviated. There was a collusion of sorts at work in their relationship. Both twins subscribed to an unspoken understanding: "You be this way, I'll be that way."

In this twinship, the noted division did not do justice to the actual talents, abilities, and interests of the twins. A further complication was the fact that the qualities that were "chosen up" in this manner and/or projected onto the twins from early on (projections with which each may have identified) were differentially valued within the family, leading to additional tensions. For example, the intellectual twin was more favored in this family, where intellectual achievement was prized and athletic ability was not. Thus, there were significant psychological ramifications to the personality traits that each twin came to adopt, with the non-intellectual twin feeling more marginalized and vulnerable within the family.

When the twins graduated from high school, the intellectual twin went on to a four-year college, while her sister stayed closer to home and attended a junior college. However, this separation provided the second twin with newfound freedom to reclaim some of the talents and abilities that had been relinquished to her sister as part of the tacit, if unconscious, agreement on dividing up personality traits. Suddenly, the twin who had been viewed as non-intellectual found herself blossoming academically. She achieved exceptional grades and eventually transferred to a prestigious four-year university. Her sister, meanwhile, had started to founder upon entering college. The separation from her twin meant the loss of a vital, needed psychological resource upon which she had unconsciously relied. There was a loss of support for an important element of this twin's internalized self representation. As a result, her grades plummeted and eventually she dropped out of college. This came as a great surprise to the family, which had always viewed her as the stronger, more independent, and more intellectual twin.

In such complementary relationships, where qualities are divided up between the twins, there is a balance struck, a kind of equilibrium attained. Unconsciously, each twin participates in the relinquished qualities and traits through identifications with the twin sibling and the vicarious experiencing that such strategies afford. So long as both members of the pair participate in this arrangement, there can be a functionality to it that works. However, it is an arrangement that requires the maintenance of the pair, and hence an arrangement that strongly reinforces unconscious intertwin identifications. It is also an arrangement that invites a rich range of unconscious fantasy and, not uncommonly, conflict. The twins may unconsciously experience themselves as a male-female couple, for example, or one may not feel psychologically complete when his or her twin is absent or when one of them deviates from the prescribed roles which they have tacitly agreed to play for themselves and for others.

The second major feature of twinning reactions and the failure to establish adequate self-object differentiation is a propensity toward regressive blurring of boundaries between the twins. For example, many twins, including the two reported on by Joseph and Tabor, report that they think of themselves as "we" not "I." As a corollary to these deficits, twins frequently evidence notable levels of dependency and separation anxiety.

For example, in Joseph and Tabor's material, twin A felt lost when separated from his "cock and balls" (as he referred to his twin brother). These characteristics were also not necessarily firmly entrenched: when the twins went off to college, occasioning their first real separation, would-be active, independent twin B was sufficiently unhappy that he joined twin A at his college after their first year, and later, when twin A entered the Army, twin B left college to join him. However, it was A who felt compelled to follow his brother into analysis when a state of acute anxiety drove B to seek treatment.

The extent of interidentification and the fluidity of boundaries between twins are important factors in the common twin feeling that only together do they constitute one complete person. There are powerful wishes at work to maintain the fantasy as well. The sense that they exist within a common psychological membrane, the symbiotic fantasy of oneness, is important to most twins. However, the wish to be separate, more autonomous, is also ever-present in twins' lives and the tensions produced by these two countervailing elements are pervasive. At times, both members of the twin pair want to be more separate from one another. At other times, they may both wish to accentuate or otherwise reinforce the merger fantasies of the twin relationship. As in all development, the dual urges toward separation-individuation and symbiosis and merger are constantly at play and are a constant source of ambivalence for twins. When the twins do not coincide in their positions on these constellations, separation anxiety, depression, and aggression are frequent by-products.

One identical twin in his mid-thirties whom I saw in treatment reported the following experience to illustrate the felt breakdown of this sense of a common bond and shared identity with his twin brother. Both of the twins were writers who for years had worked on their writing assignments together. Both were married and had two children each, with the two families sharing a duplex where they had established a kind of twin cooperative. Until well into his treatment, virtually all of my patient's professional writing efforts had been in tandem with his brother. He had never worked independently as a writer. Now, for the first time, the twins were writing separate projects, the nature of which each would not disclose to the other. This was an anxiety-producing development for each of them. My patient had immense concerns that his work would not be good enough or adequate as a solo product, while at the same time he worried that his creativity would surpass that of his brother and would activate powerful currents of envy, feelings that might threaten a relationship that was vitally important to him. In this way, he became acutely aware of the degree of interdependence between himself and his brother, the magnitude of which he had defended against.

This twin described his recollection of the first time he felt a sense of separateness from his brother. His brother had gone on a six-week vacation alone the summer between their freshman and sophomore years in college. The twins had the custom of eating together and going for leisurely strolls after dinner, during which they would discuss ideas, especially philosophical and political topics. When his brother returned from vacation, the twins went for their usual walk, and were discussing a political issue when it became clear that they had different opinions on the matter at hand. My patient reacted with astonishment: "But this is how we've *always* thought about it," he pleaded with his brother. "We're twins, we always think the same way about these things," he said. However, his brother stuck to his position and my patient reported this as "the first time I ever felt that he and I did not share the same ideas and the same feelings about something. It felt like a real loss," he said. "I was depressed for weeks after that. It was as if something that you had always known, a frame of reference that you had always assumed would be with you, was suddenly taken away. It was the first time that I became aware of the fact that my brother and I were very, very close but we were not the same person." We can readily see in this material the consequences of the interidentification between twins.

Thus, the twinning reaction is characterized by two key elements, both of which, as Joseph and Tabor (1961) hypothesized, are a function of the interidentifications between twins, and the part fusion of self and object representations that result in the diffuseness of ego boundaries. On the one hand, we see a tendency in twins to polarize identity characteristics as a strategy for anchoring a sense of self and averting dangerous feelings of rivalry and competition. On the other hand, a propensity toward regressive blurring of boundaries between the twins leaves them feeling incomplete if they are separate from their twin siblings and is often characterized by separation anxiety and dependency.

DEVELOPMENTAL SOURCES OF TWINNING REACTIONS

Symbiosis

My own work (Ainslie 1997) and other reports in the literature suggest that certain features of the twin situation create paradigmatic psychological characteristics in the twin relationship such as the twinning reaction. A number of psychoanalytic theorists have placed inordinate emphasis on the physical similarity between identical twins to account for the psychological features of twinship. While the notion of "mirror image" is appealing, it is far from sufficient to explain the complex psychological characteristics that we find in twins. For example,

mirror studies suggest that infants are not generally able to identify themselves in the mirror until they are around 24 months
old. Yet twins begin to recognize and respond to each other's
presence within the first months of life. Early traces of separation anxiety are very much in evidence well before the time that
twins have a capacity to understand that they are mirror images of one another. In addition, conceptualizations that rely
heavily on the physical similarities between twins fail to take
into account the fact that nonidentical twins, and even fraternal opposite-sex twins, may develop similar dynamics (Glenn
1966, Orr 1941).

Twinning reactions are rooted in the unusual developmental circumstances that govern the twin relationship. It is clear
that the connection between identity formation and development is complex. Self and object representations, beginning as
inchoate sensory-motor experiences with little or no represen-
tational elements, gradually evolve into the kind of structured
internal world that gives rise to a sense of identity that is cohe-
sive and that has stability over time. Thus, how experience
becomes represented internally, giving us a sense of who we are,
is crucial to our understanding of identity confusion and related
psychological phenomena in twins.

We know that during the first year of life, optimal development is fostered by a healthy, symbiotic relationship between
mother and infant in which the mother's empathic, sensitive
contact creates a psychologically nutritive environment by
which the infant is neither excessively frustrated nor excessively
engulfed (Mahler 1967, Mahler, et al. 1975). For twins, this
symbiotic context is significantly altered. The requirements of
"good enough" parenting are much harder to live up to when
parents are faced with the demands and needs of two infants at
once. Studies of parent–child interactions comparing twins with
singleton children clearly document the fact that mothers of
twins are required to spend significantly more time on infant-
related activities (Gosher-Gottstein 1979), that twins require

more overt parental control than do singletons (both in quantity and quality of verbal exchanges), and that parents of twins are less responsive to their children's distress and bids for attention (Lytton 1980). Mothers of twins often complain that they feel drained, and that especially during the first year of life, parenting their twins is often a source of significant exhaustion and frustration (Ainslie 1997).

In addition to complications in the mother–infant relationship, a second factor affecting the character of the symbiotic period of twins (and the subsequent process of separation-individuation) is the twin relationship itself. In her classic observations of the Bert and Bill twins at the Hampstead Child Therapy Clinic, Dorothy Burlingham (1952, 1963) richly describes the early and powerful effects of the twin relationship. For example, the twins stood, rocked, walked, and slept in ever-present parallel position to one another. The intensity of this relationship for each twin was reflected in both the libidinal and aggressive aspects of their interactions. Burlingham notes that from the time the twins first began to take notice of each other they showed signs of affection toward one another. "They tried to touch each other's faces, hold each other's arms and legs," she writes (Burlingham 1963). "Bert would bite Bill very gently and repeat this affectionately, and he would rub up against him . . . . Bert would often try to comfort Bill when he cried and would try to distract him (16 months). . . . When put to bed in the shelter, their bunks separated by a partition, they would talk to each other excluding all the other children" (pp. 371–372). Capturing this same quality in the twin relationship, Leonard (1961) described a set of twin infants who, while sleeping in the same crib, were repeatedly found sucking on one another's hands.

Burlingham's (1963) reports of the aggressive elements in Bert and Bill's relationship were just as prominent and started at an early age. Even as babies they were competitive, each naturally wanting to get hold of whatever the other was holding. They wrestled, hit, and screamed until one let go, angry, frustrated, and crying. Their rivalry started as soon as they became aware of each other. It extended to other areas also. For example, when one twin was fed first, the other wanted to be fed as well. According to Burlingham, each also wanted whatever the other twin possessed, be it material objects or developmental achievements. In Burlingham's view, this circumstance was a great impetus to their learning. Both twins were able to do the same things at almost the same time.

Reflecting the observations I've noted above regarding the complications in the early twin–mother relationship, Burlingham (1963) noted that "In the relationship to the visiting mother the rivalry was at its height, both demanding impatiently and passionately to be picked up and loved at the same moment. They would hit and push away the rival so as to get the mother and hit and bite the mother because she was not able to respond to both. As a result both twins would end up on the floor frustrated, screaming, and in a temper tantrum" (p. 371).

While Burlingham's observations of these twins, in the context of a residential treatment setting where they were separated from their mother at an early age, might not be taken as representative of twins in general, the fact is that most mothers of twins report similar, if less acute, processes at work. What is evident from this material is the extent to which twins are vital, potent objects in each other's psychological environment from the time that they develop an awareness of one another, an awareness that is already well in evidence by the time the twins are 5 or 6 months of age (Leonard 1961). These observations are in keeping with those of Neubauer (1983), Leichtman (1985), and Parens (1988) who note that infants form meaningful relationships even with non-twin siblings by the middle of their first year.

An added complication for twins' development is the fact that the environment within which they are growing up frequently places significant pressure on them, treating them as a unit, confusing their identities, and rewarding them for behaviors and activities that emphasize the blurring of boundaries between the two members of the pair. One mother of twins, for example, described the following: "One morning I responded to one baby's cries, brought her into bed and nursed her and played with her. Then I discovered she was not whom I thought [she was] . . . It was a very strange feeling" (Ainslie 1997, p. 34). Such confusions may have a profound impact, especially if they are an ongoing feature of a child's experience.

The increased level of frustration that is often an inherent part of the twin relationship is reflected in mothers of twins' accounts of their inability to adequately respond to the needs of their twins. Many mothers, for example, describe feeling impotent and frustrated themselves when both of their infants are crying at the same time (not an uncommon occurrence) and they can only respond to them individually, which means that one of the twins is left to cry until the caretaking task at hand is sufficiently accomplished to free the mother to respond to the second twin. A related problem is the fact that even identical twins may differ in their patterns of feeding, sleeping, and so on. Mothers of twins are faced with the unusual task of needing to synchronize themselves to the needs of two infants simultaneously, potentially creating unique psychological strains for the mothers (Escalona 1963). Many parents of twins endeavor to "economize" their efforts by keeping their twins on the same schedule. However, such a schedule may not reflect the more innate or natural rhythms of one or another twin. Such challenges are reflected in maternal reports in which mothers of twins attest to feeling that they do not think that they "know" their twins, as infants, in the way that they knew their singleton children.

In sum, the challenges of parenting twins simultaneously represents both a quantitative problem (caring for two infants at once) and a qualitative problem (being adequately attuned to each of the twins). This mixture of constant demands and exhaustion taxes the maternal capacities of even the most dedicated parent of twins. In turn, as twins begin to become aware of one another during the first year of life, parents, for these same reasons, may feel a significant measure of relief at the developing twin–twin relationship, fostering or accentuating it as a respite from the parenting challenges that they have endured.

Mahler (1967, 1968, Mahler et al. 1975) suggested that when children have not spent sufficient time alone with their mother within the symbiotic orbit, they may be left with insufficient ego resources with which to effectively meet the rigors of separation-individuation. The circumstance of twinship significantly alters the usual conditions governing a child's passage through symbiosis in preparation for separation-individuation.

Rapprochement

We know that for every child the experiences attendant to the unfolding process of separation and individuation are entertained with a significant measure of ambivalence. The urge toward experiences that underscore a sense of independence and autonomy may be a source of pleasure and delight ("the world is my oyster") while simultaneously evoking feelings of anxiety and concern (Mahler et al. 1975). The ubiquitous emergence of transitional phenomena as the process of separation-individuation is beginning to take hold stands as testimony to the stressful nature of this transition for all children, even those growing up under ideal circumstances. During rapprochement and rapprochement crisis, when these countervailing feelings reach their peak, crucial steps toward identity structuralization are taken, in the form of increasingly stable and richly diversified self- and object-representations as the child successfully engages, absorbs, and comes to terms with the conflicting forces that are at play during separation-individuation. Such an attainment is reflected in a variety of accomplishments, including greater stability of self- and object-representations, language development, impulse control, and better reality testing, among other ego functions. However, these require the successful relinquishment of more regressive symbiotic wishes, a success that is significantly ushered in by the boundary setting and appropriate frustrations introduced or brought to bear by maternal objects.

Modell's (1968) discussion of relationships that serve a transitional function emphasizes the idea that differences between the self and the object are minimized, with the object not acknowledged as being fully separate from the self. Such a circumstance has obvious implications for twin identity concerns. To the extent that twins comfort and soothe one another, to the extent that each other's presence dilutes the anxieties inherent in early development, the transitional aspects of the twin relationship are enhanced. Twins become, to varying degrees, substitutes for the maternal environment and receptacles for a variety of unconscious mutual projections and identifications organized around needs and conflicts. Differences between self and object may be minimized for each twin, or else artificially created and then undone via their mutual interidentification, with neither member of the twin pair being acknowledged as fully separate from the other.

As I have described elsewhere (Ainslie 1997), such a circumstance becomes reflected in a variety of behavioral manifestations, including twinning reactions, that are clearly in evidence by the end of the first year onward, taking different forms and characteristics as they are mediated by the vicissitudes of development over time. Thus, twins may develop indications of marked dependency and separation anxiety, for example, as well as other signs that they have developed deep interidentifications that govern their experience of themselves and others.

Such ties cement the twinship psychologically for both twins as they become primary actors in each other's emotional lives. However, twinship differs from a child's tie to transitional objects in important respects. Unlike the transitional object, one does not have complete control over one's twin, who may not be as cooperative in accepting projections and being used in the service of internal conflicts and anxieties. Twins also do not outgrow one another in the sense that children outgrow transitional objects.

The heightened tensions of the rapprochement crisis lead to an increased transitional use of the twin relationship as a means of managing anxiety. The twins' inclination to use each other as ever-present soothers and comforters may be reinforced by parental objects who, emerging exhausted out of the throes of the first two years of their twins' lives, may feel relieved that the twins are finally more able to play and otherwise entertain each other. In this way, parents may unwittingly foster greater interidentification between the twins, thereby diluting their efficacy as guides through the separation-individuation process. Not coincidentally, many theorists point out that it is during this juncture in development that twins begin to use the twin-ship defensively (e.g., Burlingham 1952, 1963, Joseph 1961).

This altered situation gives the psychological organization of twins certain common characteristics, specifically, a strong tendency toward interidentification and concomitant self-object confusion, dependency, separation anxiety, and role complementarity. The hallmarks of the so-called twinning reaction tend to be pervasive.

CLINICAL MATERIAL

Mrs. C. was a 40-year-old opposite-sex fraternal twin at the time she began three-times-per-week treatment, presenting as notably depressed with significant narcissistic conflicts. Prior to the start of first grade, the twins had been separated when Mrs. C.'s brother was held back to repeat kindergarten. In Mrs. C.'s large family the boys were prized. She described herself as a tomboy while growing up, a feature of her psychology that was overdetermined, reflecting as it did how she felt about the fact that she was female, as well as the fact that males were more greatly esteemed within the family. However, Mrs. C.'s childhood tomboyish qualities also reflected a powerful identification with her twin brother.

Shortly after leaving home for college, a significant separation from her family and from her twin brother, Mrs. C. met and quickly married an intelligent man who was more assertive in the outside world than he was at home, where she dominated. When the couple had their first child, a boy, Mrs. C. became closely and exclusively attached to him. Unconsciously, she felt rejoined with her lost twin. Throughout his childhood this boy was Mrs. C.'s "special" child, despite the fact that she had additional children. Mrs. C. noted that she felt a unique bond with him, which she ascribed to his being her firstborn child. When her son entered adolescence, his efforts to separate from Mrs. C. stirred considerable anxiety, depression, and anger in her. She was highly identified with him and she made every effort to control and subdue him as he started to separate from the family. Mrs. C.'s attempts at controlling her son served only to incite him further, and the boy became more actively confrontational and rebellious, creating familial tensions that eventually landed her in treatment.

Although initially she described only in passing the fact that she was a twin, eventually Mrs. C. came to understand the importance of her twin brother in her emotional life and to reexperience her sense of loss when she was separated from him at the beginning of first grade, when her twin was paired up with their younger brother, thirteen months their junior. Mrs. C.'s twin and her younger brother developed a twin-like relationship, doing everything together. Teachers and classmates frequently thought of them as "the twins" and treated them accordingly, which only accentuated Mrs. C.'s feeling that she had lost a twin and her younger brother had gained one. Those two siblings retained a twin-like closeness into adulthood, while Mrs. C.'s relationship with her twin brother faltered and was marked by estrangement and distance.

Mrs. C. was a statuesque, attractive woman who dressed to perfection. She had a good sense for the details of fashion, and was keenly attuned to these aspects of femininity. Her striking good looks enabled her to have a successful modeling career. However, there was a cold, phallic-narcissistic quality to this aspect of her character, which only softened after a number of years of treatment. In her modeling work, for example, she often took a "masculine" approach to her fellow models, telling them how they should look, making suggestions about their appearance, and otherwise "dressing" or directing them.

Mrs. C. was immensely ambivalent about men. While on the surface she had a highly elaborated sense of femininity, she also felt angry at men who admired her. She alternated between dressing to entice, inviting male interest and attention, and feeling resentful at being seen as an "object." Thus, she simultaneously sought to interest men and rebuff them, seduce and castrate them, all in the service of unconscious pleasure in controlling them.

While such conflicts have obvious referents to familiar issues in female development (Tyson and Tyson 1990), and in particular to her unconscious fantasies about the implications of the anatomical differences between men and women (features of her treatment that are less central to the purposes of this presentation), it was also evident that for Mrs. C. these concerns spoke to the developmental implications of being an opposite-sex fraternal twin. As her treatment progressed it became clear that Mrs. C. felt immense resentment at having lost her twin brother and she sought to both retaliate for this abandonment and ensure that it would not be repeated. She felt like an incomplete person without her twin, and she believed that he had abandoned her, in part because she was female. Thus, she unconsciously devalued the very notion of femininity, and attempted to mask her own femininity under a hardened narcissistic facade and via a phallic identification through which she sought to control both men and women.

In her treatment, a very quick transference developed (a feature that has been noted by others who have treated twins; see Joseph 1961), initially organized around maternal and twin issues. From the start she experienced my office and her sessions as a comforting enclosure. She reveled in what she felt was an exclusive maternal connection. Mrs. C. loved the silence, which she distinguished from the constant chaos of her childhood home as well as her present home, where she was the only female surrounded by her male children and her husband. Thus, in her sessions she secretly felt that finally she had her mother to herself, or, alternately, that she and her brother had been rejoined and there were no disruptions or intrusions into the closeness. Later, anxieties and resentments about my other patients, unconscious siblings who broke the fantasied exclusivity of our time, would surface and be explored.

A significant transference theme was the hope that I would make her complete. Often during this period she repeated the fantasy that she needed a man to make her complete, in order to feel like a whole person, material that was dominated by more fundamental issues regarding her identity consolidation. At this time Mrs. C. reported how she relished taking warm and leisurely baths with her husband, during which they would have intercourse, thereby recreating a fantasy of her and her twin brother, within an intrauterine enclosure, as two parts of a whole. This material also reflected the unconscious fantasy that the twins had been unevenly split (a common fantasy among opposite-sex fraternal twins; see Glenn 1966). This transference material was organized around the early twin experience that the other is necessary for the self to feel complete.

For Mrs. C. being an opposite-sex fraternal twin was rife with powerful emotional consequences. She felt incomplete without her twin brother. She had attempted to manage these concerns via a strong identification with him as a child, by becoming a tomboy. Later, she re-created a twin-like relationship with her husband and her son, both of whom she sought to control so that she might feel whole. Similar issues were repeated in the transference over the course of her treatment. To be sure, the fact Mrs. C. was a twin does not account for every feature of her psychology, and many of the dynamics I have described were multiply determined. However, it is evident that her twin brother was one of the primary organizing relationships in the course of her development. Further, the material illustrates the establishment of twinning reactions between Mrs. C.'s brother and their younger sibling (they became the "official" twins of the family), as well as her propensity to establish twin-like relationships with her husband, her son, and, in the transference, with me.

TWINNING REACTIONS IN NON-TWIN SIBLINGS

Virtually every theorist who has discussed the characteristics of twinning reactions has noted that they are not exclusively a feature of twin relationships (Joseph and Tabor 1961, Leonard 1961, Sharpe and Rosenblatt 1994, Shopper, 1974). While twins represent the clearest and perhaps the most common form, Joseph and Tabor (1961) suggest that twinning reactions are "not uncommonly encountered in other patients who are not identical twins, not even fraternal twins, not even necessarily siblings . . . this reaction may occur in siblings who are relatively close together in age, or it may be encountered, for example, between a husband and wife who have been married for a period of time" (p. 277). Similar or related phenomena have been reported in the psychoanalytic literature for years. Helene Deutsch's (1938) observations in "Folie à Deux," for example, speak to a twin-like loss of self–object differentiation between two individuals. Greenacre (1958) described what she called "pseudotwinning" in similar terms, especially noting the complications of such processes in the successful consolidation of what today we would term gender identity. Anna Freud and

Dann (1951) indicated that children who had to grow up in the concentration camps without parents were prone to developing twin-like psychological characteristics. Finally, Erikson (1968) spoke of circumstances wherein siblings were "apt to attach themselves to one brother or sister in a way resembling the behavior of twins . . ." (p. 137).

How are we to understand twinning reactions in non-twin siblings and other relationships? In what is most likely the first paper ever specifically speaking to twinning reactions in non-twin siblings, Shopper (1974) argues that children who are born two years or less apart from each other are vulnerable to developing such reactions. He emphasized the way in which parents are likely to foster the twinning reaction by treating the close-in-age siblings as if they were a pair, either in ministering child care (eating, napping, bathing) or in misguided efforts to short-circuit potential rivalrous feelings by treating the children equally or identically. Shopper argues that the closer siblings are in age, "the more they approach a state of twinship" (p. 302), the easier it is for the parents to treat them like twins.

A look at the emerging literature on non-twin sibling relations, where we find many elements typically ascribed to the twinning reaction in reference to ordinary siblings, suggests that the spacing of siblings, while an important variable, is insufficient to account for the characteristics of the so-called twinning reaction. Parens (1988), for example, invoking the functions that transitional objects play in the lives of children (Winnicott 1953), suggests that siblings "often become bridging or connecting objects between the self and the parents, and between the family and the social [object and group]" (p. 48). Similarly, Sharpe and Rosenblatt (1994), in their discussion of unresolved oedipal sibling relationships, note the "continued idealization or devaluation of a sibling . . . and the continuation of a polarization of roles and traits between or among siblings" (p. 508). These, or course, are some of the prototypical features that have been used to delineate the twinning reaction. Joseph and

Tabor (1961) suggested that twinning reactions could even be found in marital relationships. Kernberg's (1991) discussion of the psychodynamics of many marital couples and other adult intimate relationships would appear to support this observation.

One cannot help but wonder if the concept of twinning reaction begins to lose its utility as it is stretched to cover such a broad range of relational contexts and circumstances. Perhaps twinning reactions are not so much about twins as they are about the consequences of close relationships, where strong libidinal and aggressive components are at play, and where there is considerable interidentification secondary to that closeness (see Parens, this volume). It may be that the circumstance of twinship, because of the saliency of these characteristic dynamics within their relationships, brings such consequences into relief. However, it is likely that all sibling relationships, whether or not they are twins, lend themselves to similar processes given sufficient intensity. Such intensity promotes efforts to manage a variety of feelings between siblings in classic twin fashion. For example, competitive and rivalrous feelings in non-twin siblings may readily be handled via the polarization's of identity characteristics or by developing differential identifications with each of the parental objects (Shopper 1974). Variables such as proximity in age and parental conscious and unconscious attitudes as well as rearing practices all have a role in influencing such outcomes. However, it appears that what was initially viewed primarily as a twin phenomenon may be considerably more widespread. Hartmann's admonition (1934–1935) not to ascribe to the twinship every psychological issue identified in a twin takes on new meaning here.

As our understanding of sibling relationships becomes more sophisticated, and, perhaps, as it becomes less dominated by formulaic views (for example, that the depiction of siblings in psychoanalytic work is to be understood primarily as a displacement for parental objects), our understanding of the impact of siblings on development becomes accessible to a more complex rendering. Such a shift in our appreciation of the importance of sibling relationships, twin or otherwise, allows for our exploration of the impact of siblings across the span of development, including separation-individuation (Leichtman 1985, Parens 1988), oedipal development (Sharpe and Rosenblatt 1994), and adolescence (Balsam 1988). It also permits a more sophisticated understanding of the subtle ways in which sibling realities infiltrate our clinical work in the form of sibling transferences (Graham 1988) and our understanding of later object choice (Abend 1984).

REFERENCES

Abend, S. M. (1984). Sibling love and object choice. *Psychoanalytic Quarterly* 53:425–430.

Ablon, S., Harrison, A., Valenstein, A., and Gifford, S. (1986). Special solutions to phallic-aggressive conflicts in male twins. *Psychoanalytic Study of the Child* 41:239–258. New Haven, CT: Yale University Press.

Ainslie, R. C. (1997). *The Psychology of Twinship*. Northvale, NJ: Jason Aronson.

Arlow, J. (1960). Fantasy systems in twins. *Psychoanalytic Quarterly* 29:175–199.

Athanassiou, C. (1986). A study of the vicissitudes of identification in twins. *International Journal of Psycho-Analysis* 67:329–335.

Balsam, R. (1988). On being good: the internalized sibling with examples from late adolescent analyses. *Psychoanalytic Inquiry* 8:66–87.

Burlingham, D. (1952). *Twins: A Study of Three Pairs of Identical Twins*. New York: International Universities Press.

—— (in co-operation with Arthur Barron) (1963). A study of identical twins. *Psychoanalytic Study of the Child* 18:367–423.

Deutsch, H. (1938). Folie à deux. *Psychoanalytic Quarterly* 7:307–318.

Erikson, E. H. (1968). *Identity and the life cycle. [Psychological Issues, Monograph 1]*. New York: International Universities Press.

Escalona, S. (1963). Patterns of experience and the developmental process. *Psychoanalytic Study of the Child* 8:197–244. New York: International Universities Press.

Freud, A., and Dann, S. (1951). An experiment in group upbringing. *Psychoanalytic Study of the Child* 6:127–168. New York: International Universities Press.

Glenn, J. (1966). Opposite sex twins. *Psychoanalytic Quarterly* 34:636–638.

—— (1974). Twins in disguise: a psychoanalytic essay on *Sleuth* and *The Royal Hunt of the Sun*. *Psychoanalytic Quarterly* 43:288–302.

Gosher-Gottstein, E. R. (1979). Families of twins: a longitudinal study of coping. *Twins: Newsletter of the International Society for Twin Studies* 4–5:2.

Graham, I. (1988). The sibling object and its transferences: alternate organizer of the middle field. *Psychoanalytic Inquiry* 8:88–107.

Greenacre, P. (1958). Early physical determinants in the development of the sense of identity. *Journal of the American Psychoanalytic Association* 6:612–627. New York: International Universities Press, 1971.

Hartmann, H. (1934–1935). Psychiatric studies on twins. *Essays in Ego Psychology*, pp. 419–445. New York: International Universities Press, 1964.

Joseph E. (1961). The psychology of twins. *Journal of the American Psychoanalytic Association* 9:58–66.

Joseph, E., and Tabor, J. (1961). The simultaneous analysis of a pair of identical twins and the twinning reaction. *Psychoanalytic Study of the Child* 16:275–299. New York: International Universities Press.

Kernberg, O. (1976). *Object Relations Theory and Clinical Psychoanalysis.* New York: Jason Aronson.

—— (1991). Aggression and love in the relationship of the couple. *Journal of the American Psychoanalytic Association* 39(1):45–70.

Leichtman, M. (1985). The influence of an older sibling on the separation-individuation process. *Psychoanalytic Study of the Child* 40:111–161. New Haven, CT: Yale University Press.

Leonard, M. (1961). Problems in identification and ego development in twins. *Psychoanalytic Study of the Child* 16:300–320. New York: International Universities Press.

Lytton, H. (1980) *Parent–Child Interaction: The Socialization Process Observed in Twin and Singleton Families.* New York: Plenum.

Mahler, M. (1967). On human symbiosis and the vicissitudes of individuation. *Journal of the American Psychoanalytic Association* 15:740–763.

—— (1968). *On Human Symbiosis and the Vicissitudes of Individuation. Vol. 1: Infantile Psychosis.* New York: International Universities Press.

—— (1972). The rapprochement subphase of the separation-individuation process. *Psychoanalytic Quarterly* 41:487–506.

Mahler, M., Pine, F., and Bergman, A. (1975). *The Psychological Birth of the Human Infant.* New York: Basic Books.

Modell, A. H. (1968). *Object Love and Reality. An Introduction to a Psychoanalytic Theory of Object Relations.* New York: International Universities Press.

Neubauer, P. (1983). The importance of the sibling experience. *Psychoanalytic Study of the Child* 38:325–336. New Haven, CT: Yale University Press.

Orr, D. (1941). A psychoanalytic study of a fraternal twin. *Psychoanalytic Quarterly* 10:284–296.

Parens, H (1988). Siblings in early childhood: some direct observational findings. *Psychoanalytic Inquiry* 8: 31–50.

Prall, R. C. (1990). The neurotic adolescent. In *The Neurotic Child and Adolescent*, ed. M. H. Etezady, pp. 241–302. Northvale, NJ: Jason Aronson.

Sharpe, S. A., and Rosenblatt, A. (1994). Oedipal sibling triangles. *Journal of the American Psychoanalytic Association* 42:491–523.

Shopper, M. (1974). Twinning reaction in nontwin siblings. *Journal of the American Academy of Child and Adolescent Psychiatry* 13(2)300–318.

Tyson, P., and Tyson, R. L. (1990) *Psychoanalytic Theories of Development.* New Haven, CT: Yale University Press.

Winnicott, D. W. (1953). Transitional objects and transitional phenomena: a study of the first not-me possession. *International Journal of Psycho-Analysis* 34:89–97.

3

TWINS AND OTHER SIBLINGS

Discussion of Ainslie's Chapter "Twinship and Twinning Reactions in Siblings"

Henri Parens, M.D.

For many years, my patients, adults and children alike, had made me aware that their siblings have played and continue to play, to a greater or lesser degree, a meaningful part in their lives. In fact, I have found that the absence of siblings in only-child families leaves its mark as well. And having been a father for years, closely watching how our second son adored his older brother, despite the fact that his older brother at times would make it clear that life without his baby brother would be just fine, and then seeing how our third child attended to and was ever responsive to his older brothers, confirmed my clinical finding that siblings matter a great deal to us. To be sure, as is the case in all families, for our own children it was a mixed blessing. This was mostly so for our firstborn who had lived in a universe for nearly two years during which he did not need to share his parents with any uninvited—as far as he was concerned—sibling.

My wife and I see this now in our five grandchildren where, in the two sets of two siblings among them, when 1-year-old Arthur is fussy, 5-year-old Elliot can simply make an amusingly funny sound and Arthur, enchanted, will break into a big smile. And similarly, when 1-year-old Ben, eating in his high chair, sees 3-year-old Sophie walk into the kitchen, he pauses for a moment and gets this marvelous smile on his face. Of course, we have also seen 1-year-old Arthur gleefully crash one of Elliot's building constructions, for which Elliot, up to the gills with this little unasked-for sibling, walloped him one that sent the little one tumbling. In turn, this earned the 5-year-old a firmly administered scolding and a time-out, which he served with the guilt and remorse of the most contrite breaker of the law.

DIRECT OBSERVATIONAL FINDINGS ON SIBLINGS

All this I came to learn over the years. But the impact of the depth of meaning of siblings for the child, the meaningfulness of siblings as specific and primary love/hate objects, and as bridging (or linking) objects, and the part they play that can positively or negatively serve the child's development and adaptation—all this I only came to recognize by seeing it from the researcher's optimal distance, and cataloguing and weighing its value in the course of direct observational research (Parens 1988). Like Dr. Ainslie and a handful of other analysts, including Rosemary Balsam and especially Vamik Volkan, I too came to recognize the unique importance of siblings, not just as representatives or substitutes for mother and father, but as primary loved and hated objects in and of themselves.

We have defined primary objects or primary relationships as those object relations which, when we lose such an object, evoke and require of us a mourning process in order to master the loss (Parens et al. 1997). These, of course, include our mothers, fathers, mates, children, grandchildren, and grandparents when they are highly emotionally invested. Siblings also commonly form such primary relationships. We have no doubt all heard of siblings who invest large loads of hostile destructiveness in one another and hate each other, and in more troubled circumstances do not talk to each other for years. But as a father I can tell you that one of the great satisfactions I have is that our three sons, husbands and fathers themselves, have each other. I derive pleasure in knowing that our sons will be together as a widening family network, will have each other in primary relatedness for more years in the course of their lives than they will with anyone else, including their mother and me, their own mates, and their own children.

Psychoanalysis continues to enlarge our knowledge and understanding of psychic life as we add this chapter, the study of siblings, to our already vast investigation of the large and multifaceted influences of the child's relationships to his/her mother and father for the child's core personality development and adaptation. Pushing the boundaries of our explorations to address the role of siblings takes us into an arena that also independently contributes importantly to the child's development. Perhaps it is not as central and organizing as the part played by the parents, but we do find that many perhaps less central factors impact importantly on psychic development. That many factors influence psychic development probably accounts for our finding in the clinical situation that our patients are remarkably unique. In fact each is so unique that a clinical analytic approach specifically tailored to the individual patient is required. The same analytic principles apply to all, but the specific technical steps I take, the specific therapeutic procedures, are determined by multiple unique psychic features in each patient. Over the years, as I am sure is the case with all therapists, I have found my patients to be so similar, yet so different. I wonder if it might be so because the number of possible permutations of what we already know is so large. But may it not also be that there are still insufficiently appreciated forces at play in the psyches of our patients? I think the role siblings play in our patients' lives may be such an insufficiently acknowledged and detailed force.

ON TWINS

In his study, Dr. Ainslie is looking at a most fascinating and unique human condition and state: that of being a twin. I think it turns into a very useful study in contrasts or in distinctions. As with all good studies of contrasts, be it health versus pathology, childhood versus adulthood, femaleness versus maleness, the study of contrast is known to further highlight the inherent nature of things. Newborns are drawn to stare at lines of contrast. There is a built-in tendency in us to explore contrasts. It may be the most informing first step toward learning about something still unknown. Dr. Ainslie's examination of some distinctiveness of twins, specifically the "twinning reaction" (Joseph and Tabor 1961), unavoidably takes us into an area of contrast: differences between twin and non-twin siblings. Because it is helping me understand both better, I want to dissect my way through some of Dr. Ainslie's elegant report.

Dr. Ainslie notes that "virtually every theorist who has discussed the characteristics of twinning reactions has noted that they are not exclusively a feature of twin relationships" (this volume, p. 46). I agree with Dr. Ainslie that if this is so, then we are stretching the concept beyond its utility. With all due respect for Joseph and Tabor (1961), Leonard (1961), Shopper (1974), and Sharpe and Rosenblatt (1994), I would say then that what are described are not twinning reactions but rather sibling reactions that also occur in twins.

Looking very closely at twins we have found important development-influencing factors that exist in the much larger population. The important factors ascribed to the powerful experience of being a twin are actually found much more commonly than initially assumed and in ordinary siblings, not just in twins. I am certain that there are twin-specific features that probably do distinguish them from other sibships. Here's what I mean.

In direct observations I have not found that identity assignment or a polarization of identity characteristics occurs more commonly in twins than in non-twin siblings. It is my impression that such distribution of family characteristics occurred as much in the non-twin sibling population of our project as it did in the four sets of twins I now have in my mind's eye, only one set of which was in our observational project population (Parens 1979). Depending on the pressure of their proclivities to do this, parents unavoidably tend to more or less assign identity characteristics to their children not only once they can be visualized in presentation and in behaviors, but prebirth, and perhaps even prior to conception. Once into our atmosphere, "He's just like his father!" is only too commonly part of the neonate's early verbalized identity assignments. Parents are influenced in doing so, among other factors, by the complement of their own intrapsychically determined, idealized, self-fulfilling, or replacement needs on the one hand and, on the other hand, by the infant's own biogenetic dispositions and behavioral tendencies. These identity assignments occur, I have found, just as much with non-twin siblings as with twins. I would say that it is more determined by the parents than the children. To the degree that they become self-assigned, here too I am not certain that they occur more among twins.

However, it makes much sense to me that, as Dr. Ainslie and other colleagues assert, there are "twinning reactions." Like Ainslie, I find very plausible Joseph and Tabor's finding of the tendency more commonly among twins than in other siblings. This reaction "consists of: (1) mutual interidentification, and (2) part fusion of the self-representation and the object-representation of the other member of the pair" (Joseph and Tabor 1961, p. 277). It certainly would follow, as these authors propose, that both factors would lead to "a diffuseness of ego boundaries between the twins" (Ainslie, this volume, p. 29). Today, for the sake of clarity, I would say of the latter statement that it leads to a blurring of *self* boundaries between the twins, limiting the concept *ego* to that of the structural model of the mind (Hartmann 1952).

In addition, it seems to me that the search for specific twinning effects might best be found exactly where Dr. Ainslie has been looking. I agree with him that the "physical similarity between identical twins . . . is far from sufficient to explain the complex psychological characteristics that we find in twins" (this volume, p. 35). And I think he hit brilliantly on the strategy of looking at how the major early developmental processes, separation-individuation and Oedipus complex evolution, might be influenced by twinning. He is right to look there because twins travel the pathways of development along two major experiential parameters that distinguish them from non-twin siblings: they travel (1) in remarkably close proximity of space, place, and time, as if in the same canoe. Twins probably spend more time with one another there than either they or their other siblings spend with their mother or each other. And (2) they travel their odyssey in this canoe, much closer than do other siblings, within the same objectal and emotional-psychological environment—the crucible of the child's personality formation, the same way that mother and father are then in the same time era of their own lives, in the same emotional-psychological frame and space, other siblings being the same in their own respective emotional-psychological development, time frame, and space, and so on. What I am referring to here is that parents and children all evolve over time. Parents are not altogether the same parents along all parameters with all their children. Of course, parents react variably to each child, including the twins, but more to my point is that their lives change over time: their work progressions change, their economic status changes, their emotional lives change, family strains change. They are just not the same in 1999 as they were in 1994. Furthermore, parents are not the same with their firstborn as they are with their second-born, and certainly they are not the same with their twins as they are with their singletons. In this then, twins, more than other siblings, are much more in the same canoe, going down the same river, on the same day, under the same environmental and holding-environmental conditions, including also the degree to which mother and father are uniquely challenged by the stresses of rearing twins, a point duly emphasized by Ainslie.

There is another factor that distinguishes twins from other siblings. They start their life journey together well before other siblings do.

TWINS' INTRAUTERINE BEGINNINGS

For a moment let us push the boundaries of our usual analytic domain. As we contemplate the factors that influence how twins come to interidentify and blur self- and object-representations, we can speculate on the possible consequences that arise from the fact that they really start their life journey together well before they come to occupy cribs in the same room, well before they get to see their own mothers, fathers, and siblings. Some among us, like Berry Brazelton (1981), Rachel A. Parens (1998), and others, have come to wonder whether psychological life may begin before birth. Brazelton found that third-trimester fetuses are dramatically responsive to sound and even to transabdominally aimed bright lights; they react to these events physically. It is averred by research and by parents that the fetus in utero will respond to frequently played music and when that fetus becomes a newborn, it will respond preferentially to that music. So it is also for mother's voice.

Given these findings then, would we go too far astray to propose that twins, in some precognitive reactive way, probably come to cathect their intrauterine cohort? Fraternal/sororal twins may have a thin double veil between them, but they certainly experience each other in the course of their fetal development. Can we suggest as do Brazelton, R. Parens, and others that they may do so some time in the third trimester? Perhaps they do so even earlier. And identical twins certainly get to know each other at a precognitive psychobiological level. They are in exactly the same space from time zero. Is it surprising then, that if indeed, as Freud said in 1939, "the earliest cathexes are indelible," twins might have a much greater degree of difficulty in teasing out their truly individual sense of self and in disidentifying from each other in the process of separation-individuation than might a singleton? Did identical twins especially not in fact come from the most basic oneness, the same embryo? Could there be some psychological residue from this absolute biological oneness? Let me leave this speculative line of thought and return to Dr. Ainslie's presentation.

THE REWARDING REPLICABILITY OF OBSERVATIONAL FINDINGS

Ainslie's turning to Burlingham's study is well warranted. In the 1940s Dorothy Burlingham, Anna Freud, and S. Dann were among the first to directly observe non-clinical prelatency-age children from a depth-psychological vantage point. Their work especially contributed to Kris's and Hartmann's independent urgings in 1950 for depth-psychological direct observational research.

It is rewarding to me to learn from Dr. Ainslie that, blind to Burlingham's findings, during our observational studies thirty years after Burlingham reported on her Hampstead Clinic study, our research team found and reported exactly the kinds of behaviors in our subjects as those reported by Burlingham. As I said in 1988, we too found that in their relationships siblings showed reciprocal primary object level emotional investments in both libidinal and aggressive spheres. Like Burlingham and

Ainslie, I, too, was surprised by and attempted to document the depth to which these emotional investments go.

Here are two of many events illustrative of the meaning the twins in our observation project evidenced for each other.

For reasons we could not determine, 3½-year-old Donnie surprised all of us one morning when, seemingly unprovoked, he grabbed 20-month-old Candy around the neck in a half nelson. Candy, a lovely, calm, sturdy girl with the determination of a tank, looked quite distressed. The response of the mothers and observers was immediate, with the two mothers of these children compelling Donnie to let go. Though she no doubt was furious with Donnie for this unprovoked attack, Candy reacted with somberness, moped some, and found ways to annoy her twin sister Cindy by grabbing a couple of toys with which Cindy was playing. At the next observational session three days later, Candy seemed preoccupied and sober, not altogether involved in activity. When Donnie, his mother, and younger sister came in, Candy walked up to him and with a wry smile struck him forcefully on the arm with her fist! We inferred that in the heat of the event three days earlier, the ego was overwhelmed by both the physical pain and narcissistic injury Donnie inflicted on her and by the hostile destructiveness these generated, and in a more troubled functional state, Candy simply displaced her brimming hostility onto the safest of all objects—her twin. Three days later, with the ego in a much better state, Candy seemed to have prepared herself, planned to exact retribution, and indeed effected justice (as J. Gilligan [1997] proposes) for the injury Donnie did her. On the way to this point, however, her twin got a dose of the hostility generated by and earmarked for Donnie.

But then, it was also with Cindy that Candy got herself involved in one of her earliest shows of love. Understandably concerned when things sounded more quiet than usual in their apartment, Mrs. H. went to her then 3-year-old daughters' room to find them on the bed, naked and in an embrace, playing Mom and Dad.

The problem of rivalry, that bugaboo of sibling life, can be even more intense in twins than in non-twin siblings, and the burden this adds to the parents' efforts to cope with twins is great. We have all seen the situation of two infants clamoring equally loudly for attention at the same time. The strain on the parents is enormous. But the alternatives to both clamoring at the same time can sometimes be equally problematic. For instance, in our research set of twins, the better developed twin adapted quite well, allowing Mother to first care for the smaller, irritable twin, and then making sure her claims were heard. However, in another set of twins, the clamoring twin only too successfully got the better developed twin to yield his place—though the parents unwittingly contributed to this yielding by assigning the care of the difficult twin to Mother and the more malleable and patient twin to Grandmother. The negative consequences to both twins of such handling can be substantial.

I can attest to the consensus stated by Ainslie (this volume, p. 38) that "twins are vital, potent objects in each other's psychological environment," but I would say that this is so from even earlier than when they become cognitively aware of each other. This is amply evident from about 3 months of age when we begin to see clear evidence of the beginning structuring of libidinal objects (Spitz 1965), and from the beginnings of attachment (Bowlby 1958); cognitive awareness of the other is readily observable. The degree to which the sibling becomes structured as libidinal object was dramatically illustrated by Erna Furman (1974) in her report of a 12-month-old child who seemed inexplicably to suddenly refuse to eat, and would restlessly search throughout his home (as Furman construed when called in to evaluate this infant) vainly looking for his sibling who had died a few days earlier.

We need more studies of just what Dr. Ainslie is currently (this volume) opening for us to view: the effects of the more narrowly defined "twinning factors," that is, the strong tendency toward interidentification and concomitant self-object confusion, dependency and separation anxiety, and the role of complementarity in twins' development. These are in large part the products of their being in the same canoe, traveling the same developmental processes during the same day-by-day emotional-psychological family history.

WANTING WHAT THE OTHER KID'S GOT

There is another fascinating but troublesome finding Burlingham, observing in London, and I, observing in Philadelphia (thirty years apart and blindly on my part) noted. In fact, we came upon virtually the same way of expressing this misery very young children begin to give much evidence of: wanting what the other kid's got. It has implications for our further understanding the complexity of sibling (and other) rivalries.

Having seen her two older daughters make their lives and hers miserable with their painful encounters over the same toy or cup or spoon, again and again, Mrs. H. had an idea she thought would prevent such encounters in her infant twins: she bought them exactly the same toys. It did not take long for all of us in the research setting to see that with apparent purpose, her own toy in one hand, 12-month-old Cindy approached her twin Candy—the sturdier of the two—and, seemingly fascinated with Candy's toy, grabbed it from her, to Candy's dismay. Mother was dismayed as well. We were impressed with Cindy's resolve to do something that could only lead her into trouble! Indeed, after a moment of sorting out what had just happened, calm and sturdy Candy grabbed it right back.

As I wondered in 1988, surely " 'wanting what the other kid's got' plays a significant part in some forms of sibling rivalry. . . . Somewhere . . . wanting mother's attention solely for oneself plays its large contributing part" (p. 41). I then linked it with possibly being operative in the girl's wish for a penis. "If 'the wish to have what the other kid's got' operates from about six months of age on with a remarkable degree of persistence and in most if not all [sighted] children, then this could well play a part in intensifying the wish for the visualized penis" (p. 42).

Over time I have come to think that this onerous "wish to have what the other kid's got" probably has its roots in the infant's primary narcissism (Freud 1914) and continues to plague people in the conviction that the grass is greener on the other side. It may well be that Melanie Klein came to her assumptions about the centrality of envy in the human psyche from this type of clinical and direct child observation.

To what Ainslie has detailed for us regarding the symbiosis and rapprochement, let me add a note to his observations on twins' separation-individuation process. Pointing to the child's organizing ambivalence during rapprochement, Ainslie says that twins will be thrust into "a sense of independence and autonomy [that] may be a source of pleasure and delight ('the world is my oyster') while simultaneously evoking feelings of anxiety and concern" (Ainslie, p. 40, this volume). I want to elaborate this point a bit further. Starting even before rapprochement, during the practicing subphase, the thrust to individuate, that is, to go toward independence and autonomy, evokes even more anxiety than that brought about by separation alone. The thrust to autonomy, powerfully driven from within, hand in hand with healthy narcissism, is an unavoidable generator of battles of wills and therewith of ambivalence (Parens 1979, 1989). From the thrust to autonomy instigating a greater or lesser degree of ambivalence, it manages to arouse a great deal of anxiety for many years to come.

Ainslie distinguishes twinship from what Modell (1968) describes as sibling "transitional objects." I too considered some elements of sameness between Winnicott's invaluable concept of transitional objects and phenomena and the role siblings can play in each others' lives. Both can help the child separate and individuate from the symbiotic selfobject (if I may mix models) as well as help resolve each other's oedipal attachments, though the latter may entail some risk. But, like Ainslie, I feel there are important distinctions between transitional objects and siblings.

Like Ainslie, I had much sympathy for Mrs. C. How well she was helped by the insight and empathy brought to her treatment by Dr. Ainslie! No doubt his recognition of the traumatic loss Mrs. C. experienced when she and her twin were separated at age 6, made even more painful by her witnessing her twin being entwined with their younger sibling, made it possible for her to grasp emotionally why she was so peremptorily controlling of her husband and especially her own firstborn. The pressure to reenact her twinship, to heal its rupture with her firstborn son must have been powerful, especially because he was a boy. Does this not belong to that phenomenon elsewhere described as "a replacement baby"?

In closing, I agree with Ainslie that we should hold to the narrow, specific definition of the "twinning reaction." At the same time we should further elaborate the complex and rich ways siblings, whether twin or non-twin, influence each other. Let me say here, as I did in 1988, that under average expectable conditions, siblings are on earth with each other longer than they are with any other humans, including mothers, fathers, wives, and their own children. To be sure, they will not be the most primary love objects during all those years. But although, as Drs. Volkan and Balsam have written, it may not always be so, siblings can for a long time be enormously meaningful to each other and their individual nuclear families.

REFERENCES

Bowlby, J. (1958). The nature of the child's tie to his mother. *International Journal of Psycho-Analysis* 39:350–373.

Brazelton, B. (1981). Developmental theory and separation-individuation. Paper presented at The Twelfth Margaret S. Mahler Symposium, Philadelphia PA, May.

Freud, S. (1914). On narcissism: an introduction. *Standard Edition* 14:69–102.

Furman, E. (1974). *A Child's Parent Dies: Studies in Bereavement.* New Haven: Yale University Press.

Gilligan, J. (1997). *Violence: Reflections on a National Epidemic.* New York: Vintage Books.

Hartmann, H. (1952). The mutual influences in the development of the ego and the id. *Psychoanalytic Study of the Child* 7:9–30. New York: International Universities Press.

Joseph, E., and Tabor, J. (1961). The simultaneous analysis of a pair of identical twins and the twinning reaction. *Psychoanalytic Study of the Child* 16:275–299. New York: International Universities Press.

Leonard, M. (1961). Problems in identification and ego development in twins. *Psychoanalytic Study of the Child* 16:300–320. New York: International Universities Press.

Mahler, M. S., Pine, F., and Bergman, A. (1975). *The Psychological Birth of the Human Infant.* New York: Basic Books.

Modell, A. H. (1968). *Object Love and Reality: An Introduction to a Psychoanalytic Theory of Object Relations.* New York: International Universities Press.

Parens, H. (1979). *The Development of Aggression in Early Childhood.* New York: Jason Aronson.

—— (1988). Siblings in early childhood: some direct observational findings. *Psychoanalytic Inquiry* 8:31–50.

—— (1989). Toward an epigenesis of aggression in early childhood. In *The Course of Life, Vol. 2, Early Childhood,* ed. S. I. Greenspan and G. H. Pollock, 2nd ed., pp. 689–721. New York: International Universities Press.

Parens, H., Scattergood, E., Duff, S., and Singletary, W. (1997). *Parenting for Emotional Growth: A Curriculum for Students in Grades K Thru 12. Volume 1: The Textbook* (7 Modules), and *Volume 2: The Lesson Plans* (9 Modules). Philadelphia: In-Progress printing by Parenting for Emotional Growth, Inc.

Parens, R. A. (1998). *Toward the Electra/Clytemnestra Complex: Psychoanalysis and Greek Tragedy.* Work in progress.

Sharpe, S., and Rosenblatt, A. (1994). Oedipal sibling triangles. *Journal of the American Psychoanalytic Association* 42:491–523.

Shopper, M. (1974). Twinning reactions in nontwin siblings. *Journal of the American Academy of Child & Adolescent Psychiatry* 13:300–318.

Spitz, R., with W. G. Cobliner. (1965). *The First Year of Life.* New York: International Universities Press.

4

SISTERS AND THEIR DISAPPOINTING BROTHERS

Rosemary H. Balsam, M.D.

Freud and many of his followers articulated a vision of sex, gender, and psychosexual development as seen through the lens of favored brothers looking askance at their diminished sisters. Horney (1926) famously challenged the Freudian scheme by writing, "The present analytical picture of feminine development (whether that picture be correct or not) differs in no case by a hair's breadth from the typical ideas which the boy has of the girl" (p. 327.) Females have often generated and absorbed this image of themselves, that is, a woman as seen through the eyes of a young boy. Virginia Woolf, a contemporary of Horney, in her 1929 work *A Room of One's Own*, was scathing about the childlike insults of the great Dr. Samuel Johnson, who said that a woman preaching "is like a dog walking on its hind legs. It is not done well, but you are surprised to find it done at all" (p. 54). "How much thinking those old gentlemen used to save one!" (p. 46) she declared with irony. She fantasizes a life for a pretend sister of Shakespeare she calls Judith, and concludes that indeed no woman at that time *could* have survived being creative. Judith ends up a social outcast and even commits suicide. "It needs little skill in psychology to be sure that a highly gifted girl who tried to use her gift for poetry would have been so thwarted and hindered by other people, so tortured and pulled asunder by her own contrary instincts, that she must lose her health and sanity to a certainty" (p. 49). Three centuries after Shakespeare, in gentler circumstances, one wonders what skewed view of the gendered world Freud's merely two years younger sister Anna could have had, having experienced the loss of her piano because her brother Sigmund demanded that the house be quiet to enhance his powers of concentration! *He* always had a room of his own, and also the good fortune that his parents had a fantasy that he was destined for greatness (Gay 1988). Freud's phallocentric vision of psychosexual development merely lent credence to an existent social norm. Modern psychoanalysis is still exploring gender-related phenomena of psychic life and is still struggling to settle on a theoretical picture of development that is more disinterested than past visions and more free of personalized stereotypic and biased value systems. Examples of significant modern contributions aiding this task have been the papers in the '70s through the '90s elucidating the genital phases of the girl, by Henri Parens, George Pollock, Daniel Stern, and Selma Kramer, or the work on the female superego and the maternal ego ideal by Harold Blum, authors who directly or indirectly are also connected to this book through the Margaret S. Mahler Symposium on Child Development.

THE SISTERS OF DIMINISHED BROTHERS: A CLINICAL INVESTIGATION OF REVERSING GENDER STEREOTYPING

Over the years I have noticed that a number of female patients do not at all seem to fit the stereotype of the female with low self-regard. In worldly terms, these women were among the most highly ambitious and aggressively achieving people whom I have encountered as an analyst. In this chapter I will explore some of their features.

My full sample was a group of seven women who had brothers who were very disappointing to them and to their entire families. Characteristics that these women had in common were the following: they had outstandingly easygoing relations to their direct and indirect aggression and to their attitudes about competition; the durability of their self-esteem was impressive, in spite of blows from the outside world that I fancied would have made an average person cringe; they were capable of restoring their own best image to themselves rapidly: they had a vigorous appetite for life and reported a gambler's thrill toward risk-taking in a number of areas. These were features that seemed to me very different from the stereotyped woman who is given to self-effacement, cares for and about others to a fault, and is subservient to men and fearful of aggression. The most troubled pattern showed up in their intimate sustained relationships to men. Out of seven cases, five were heterosexual in their object choice (two of these will be reported here) and two were homosexual.

These cases are interesting because the conduct of these women in the world and their worldly success are akin to the classical powerful male of old. In an earlier psychoanalytic atmosphere of the unquestioning acceptance of phallic dominance, I believe that it would have been impossible to discuss much beyond these women's so-called "phallic narcissism," a term that signifies both a female developmental stage and a state of adoration of the self as phallus. Any hint of phallic denigration by a female used to be (and often still is, in analytic circles) taken necessarily as evidence of warding off phallic envy. Yet, as with female denigration by a man, actual envy of the other sex may or may not play a significant role. For example, the desire *not* to be a boy may be as important an issue for a particular girl as any boy's desire *not* to be a girl. If one accepts the intrinsic nature of bisexuality articulated by Freud, it follows that deep ambivalence about the sexual organs is basic in mental life for both genders. Admired phallic concerns and imagery played a lesser role than might be imagined in the women's inner world of power and self-love. In addition, and in given instances for example, primitive female sex symbols can hold a similar or greater internal significance to the familiar phallus; where issues of maleness do emerge, "boy-phallic" and "man-phallic" wishes, fears, and fantasies each carry a different valence for women and can have different implications. It is oversimplifying to perceive everything male in the unconscious as adored and phallic. The lowly boys in these cases provided images of undesirable male organs, which the developing girls strove to metabolize in their internal lives.

These women acted very confidently in their worlds, as if all their wishes would be fulfilled. Had one asked them on a questionnaire about such issues, they would have described their lives as vehicles for delivering the things they wanted most. Difficulties were seen as infuriating but merely temporary obstacles that could certainly be overcome, and not as the irreparable damaging catastrophes that women who suffer from marked castration concerns typically experience. I want to explore the positive and adaptive aspects of these women's appetitive approach to life. Outstanding women who have aspired to as much success as these have been little described in our literature. Where they do appear, mostly pain and the negative aspects of their inner lives have been emphasized.

Edith Jacobson (1959) wrote a paper on a variation of a theme of Freud's, called "The Exceptions." It describes the characters and the fates of some women, including one who was exceptionally beautiful. They felt internally exempt from ordinary morality, as in Freud's interpretation of Shakespeare's *Richard III*. In consequence, Jacobson interpreted, the women exhibited a "dangerous masochistic need for punishment" (p. 139). They had to "pay dearly for not submitting to ordinary rules" (p. 153). The patient narratives are full of agony and they read like a modern morality play in which the unfortunates, because of their overweening pride, are punished for violating fundamental laws of nature (e.g., the oedipal complex). Anton Kris (1976) also wrote a paper revisiting Freud's "Exceptions," entitled "On Wanting Too Much." Although not about women per se, this paper is about insatiability and the difficult-to-detect presence of unconscious guilt in narcissism. I include this reference because narcissistic dynamics were certainly prominent in my seven analysands and a common feature was their lack of the conscious experience of guilt. Kris's paper links the lack of conscious guilt and the presence of unconscious guilt to the intolerance of passive wishes. His thesis, however, assumes marked parental deprivation in connection with his patients' insatiability. My patients do not quite fit this description. They were massively indulged as well as deprived. Except in the case of Brenda B., whose brother was dead, I did not detect the unconscious guilt that I had fully expected to be present. Another paper relevant to the topic of those with special opportunities in life is by Roy Schafer (1992), entitled "Women Lost in the Maze of Power and Rage." His successful career women repetitively enslaved themselves to victimizing men. Although I do not expand fully enough here on their problems with men to compare and contrast them to this paper, my cases seemed to me to behave like the rapacious men in Schafer's account. The damaged brother, perhaps intrapsychically, granted them permission to become guiltless victimizers. All of these papers paint rather dire pictures of the pain in the lives of these outstanding people, miserable and unfortunate in the exercise of their gifts. The ghostly legacy of Shakespeare's sister still appears to hover in the wings.

None of the subjects of my present series viewed themselves as particularly tragic on account of their reactions to their talents (cf. Jacobson 1959), or even as a result of their internal unbridled omnipotence, for example. This is, of course, separate from a societal view that might indeed find some of them morally repugnant. There is little to compare in the analytic literature that describes the internal life of extremely worldly, ambitious, or intellectually talented women (except for the pieces mentioned above, which can be criticized for not being entirely analogous). In older writing (for example, Helene Deutsch 1945), women were sometimes described as conceiving ambitions, as if above their station, or as if engagement in the work world, even for the analysands of female analysts, risked their straying into territory that was not their metier and belonged to men alone. Therefore the thrust of their energies into that world was necessarily read by the audience as male, that is, phallic. It is a sign of more modern times (such as Schafer 1992) that it is now possible for analysts to consider women's worldly function in the marketplace as important as their capacity to form relationships and/or a family. It is hoped that the phallic dimension to their dynamics, when it is present, these days is interpreted as having more to do with internal life and less with value judgment. Moreover, it is clear that phallic dynamics may be just as much a feature of a given woman's domestic life as her worldly life, and may sometimes be a minor feature in both spheres.

PRESENTATION FOR ANALYSIS

Patient A.

Ms. A. was 28 when I first met her. She briefly mentioned a young brother aged 16. He was called Teddy and was "at home with Mom" in northern New England. Her father was an international lawyer, living with his girlfriend in New York. He was divorced from the mother when the patient was 13. Ms. A. was a brilliant doctoral student in economics. She had plans for a government career and headed toward Washington on weekends and vacations from school as surely as a swallow flies south in winter. Undaunted by her student status, Ms. A. seemed to be at ease working side by side with senior figures on the political world stage. To her there was no question at all that she belonged in the company of those who design the planet. Ms. A. was of medium-slim build, athletic, and a serious intellectual. She wore black pants and elegant sweaters at all times but always included somewhere a flash of primary color in unexpected places—on a sock, or a cuff, or a lapel. While telling about her clothes she referred to the play *Master Class*, where Maria Callas as an ex-diva insists to a dowdy pupil, "You have to have a Look! Get a Look! You don't have a Look!" Ms. A felt it was vital to have a unique "look" and to show yourself and "get ahead of the pack." Her reason for seeking analysis now was because a three-year troubled relationship with a male fellow student was breaking up. She had pursued him—"hunted" him was her word—winning him away from another woman, but had never felt he was suave enough and sure enough of himself to satisfy her. He was too intimidated by her, she said.

Patient B.

Ms. B. was a portly divorced woman in her forties, who had three teenaged children and an ex-husband who was a very wealthy businessman. Her main complaint was that she was angry and felt that she could not stop her rage about her husband from overflowing onto her children. Her comments about him were demeaning and hateful. She regretted her statements, not because she had reconsidered, but because of "my poor children—he *is* their father, after all." A number of years previously she had begun a real estate business of her own in the city. With the help of all the network contacts from her family and friends she found she was doing inordinately well financially. Even in a poor market the patient turned large profits. She loved letting herself go, taking a risk, "no holds barred," she laughed. She played the real estate and stock markets to massive advantage. Ms. B. literally used to roar with laughter on the couch, often in response to some wicked fantasy to outwit her ex-husband's business associates. Ms. B. was heiress to the fortune of a wealthy and influential man and was also very philanthropic. She was adored by both parents and was close to them. She mentioned a family "sadness"—an only brother, George, with spina bifida and cerebral palsy who had died when he was 5 and she was 3. Her parents rarely talked about him and did not like to be reminded of him. She vaguely wondered how his life and death may have had some kind of impact on her.

ANALYTIC MATERIAL RELATING TO BROTHERS

Patient A.

The brother of Ms. A, the economist, was twelve years younger than she. She did not mention for months that there was anything wrong with him. There were no images in dreams that reminded her of him either. I assumed that as she was pubertal at the time of his birth, and because the divorce had occurred the following year, it would be reasonable for a sister so disturbed by these events also to be subject to immense jealousy. She might be glad to disregard him, even unconsciously. I thought of Joyce's Stephen Dedalus who said that "a brother is as easily forgotten as an umbrella." I thought that Ms. A.'s worldly sophistication and whirlwind, glamorous life also related to a need to see herself as very separate from her divorced mother, who lived in spartan fashion in Maine.

Teddy turned out to be either autistic or to have a pervasive developmental disorder. Over time I pieced the following together. The patient openly and unapologetically utterly despised him. His speech was impaired and he was demanding, loud, and stubborn. He frequently threw temper tantrums. He and Mother were totally enmeshed. Mother and Father had had screaming fights in the year after his birth. The mother was unable to soothe Teddy, who had a piercing and relentless cry. Father sent Ms. A. to boarding school when she was 14. Ms. A. consciously and unconsciously held her mother responsible for Teddy's problems. This attitude echoed her callous and unscrupulous father. Mother had had a very difficult pregnancy with Teddy when Ms. A. was 12 and pubertal. Ms. A.'s memories of the mother's pregnancy proved to be surrounded with fear and repugnance for the female body in this state. The daughter lost what little she had had of this chronically depressed mother in the pregnancy and after Teddy's birth. Boarding school and teachers helped Ms. A develop. The admired father who earlier had been absent became much more interested in her company when she entered her teenage years. This phenomenon seems to add a special zest to such a girl's spirit for achievement even if it also confuses and befuddles the internal gender identity (Balsam 1988). He was an international lawyer who began to take her on trips with him. He was charmed by her nubile youth and her intelligence. He and Ms. A. formed a loving duo from which the irritable, burdened mother was excluded. From the beginning Ms. A. was openly aggressive toward Teddy at every opportunity. She told me with little shame that she had put a pillow over his head till he turned blue. "I didn't really intend to kill him. Well, maybe I did want an accident . . . certainly I remember a lot wanting to make him cry." We gathered that hurting Mother by hurting Teddy were nearly indistinguishable from each other.

When she was a junior in boarding school and home for a vacation, Teddy, at age 4, would sometimes crawl into bed with her. She told about secretly handling his penis and delighting in seeing his erection. He was frequently enuretic, and Ms. A. dimly wondered if her sexual stimulation of him was connected. She was pleased that her father paid the boy little attention. She endlessly seemed to toy with Teddy, as if he were not quite human. I wondered if her cruelty was enhanced also by her lack of daily contact with him. She would lie on top of him and pin him down, not actually putting his penis in her vagina, but in her crotch. I asked what he would do at these times, "He often ended up crying and when he was big enough he'd say he'd tell Mom. I had him petrified." (She still laughed at the recollection, quickly covering it over by giggling— with nervousness, she said on my inquiry.) "I threatened that I'd cut his silly wee-wee off if he told on me. I don't know if he ever did. He wasn't organized enough to tell. Daddy would never have believed it anyway. He couldn't stand Teddy. And Teddy would just have told my mother and that didn't matter. What could she do?" She would stop and sigh, changing her mood for a moment." Alas, poor Teddy. I am very bad to him," she would add with little remorse. "I probably *should* feel bad . . . but Daddy says, who is to stand in judgment over anything we've experienced? It's up to us."

Patient B.

Ms. B., in contrast to Ms. A., remembered much pathos surrounding her damaged brother. Either he was never referred to in the family or else he was a point in time, a marker of the evolution of their lives, "at the time of the poor baby." The parents, who were consumed with the management of their wealth, also referred to "the time of the Depression" with the same sad affect. When the patient was angry at them as a teenager she recalled accusing them of thinking of the children as investments. Just look at what had happened in having a boy who was a bad investment, she would say to punish them. That would make them miserable and then she would become anxious and speedily cheer them up with some personal success story.

As a girl Ms. B. used to feel bad about having no available tender feelings about the dead baby. I was able to help her see that she had never known him in any whole way, as she was only 3 when he died. She was also not mature enough yet to be able to know grief. In her omnipotence that lived on vividly from that era, she thought that she *should* have known him as well as her parents. She felt terrible that as a child she would be impelled to laugh when the phrase "at the time of the poor baby" was used, and impelled to an anxious word-game associations, for example, "at the time of the flood," "at the time of Methuselah," "time and tide wait for no man," a song "dee-dee-dee-dee it's time to go-o," or "at the time of the dinosaurs." Then she would think of dinosaurs, and dinosaurs making love, and dinosaur penises, and dinosaur vaginas, and big bellies, and dinosaurs laying eggs, and she would end up screaming with laughter. We were able in retrospect to understand these emotional riffs as fraught with anxiety and fantasies of the absurdity of her parents having sex in order to create a deformed baby. "After all," she said, "it could have been me." In analysis, Ms. B. came in touch with a considerable amount of survivor guilt and many feelings about carrying the burden of the fate of the older dead sibling, trying to live for both of them to please and comfort her parents. Ms. B.'s dreams at times would be filled with deformed lumps and tumors containing hair and teeth all attached to her own body. Sometimes they would be joined at the hip. Sometimes they emerged from her anus, and sometimes from her breast or abdomen. Once she dreamed

of him as the Tar Baby from Brer Rabbit. These we understood as images of her damaged brother, blended with
terrors of the idea of pregnancy. Some of these images were
heightened further by her intense oedipal situation and
representations of Daddy's baby as a devil baby. In a dream
she also referred to herself as "Rosemary's Baby," which
represented both herself and a devil baby conceived with
mother/analyst. She recalled being fearful of giving birth
to a monster with each of her own pregnancies. As a child
she also thought that for a time she had invented an imaginary older brother, who was everything that her "poor dead
brother" could not be. His name was Prince and naturally
he was tall and handsome and accompanied her, especially
when she was lonely and sad. In the analysis her tender
yearning for a normal, older brother emerged in fantasies
about a male analysand in the waiting room. Wanting to
be both boy and girl for her parents was present, but the
wishful "boy" phallic elements were actually minor. The
small damaged penis was perceived by her as inferior to her
own genital equipment. Being a fellow grown-up along with
her parents was highly desirable as an adult male phallic
presence but especially as a giant fecund mother. The latter unconscious fantasy was the most informing of her inner world.

PARENTAL ATTITUDES

These influences are naturally exceedingly important in their
details. The feeling that one sibling has about another is inex-
tricably blended with the perceptions of how the other is treated
by each parent (Solnit 1983), the favorite parent having a different significance from the less favorite parent. The gender
input regarding highly prized traits expressed by each parent is
an important influence in mutual gender enmities between and
among siblings. I will summarize this material for these patients.

Patient A.

The mother was depressed, worn, and downtrodden, neglected by her husband and undervalued by both daughter
and husband. Her solace was the disturbed Teddy, and she
alternately "loved him to death" with smothering activities
or screamed at his out-of-control behavior in frustration.
Ms. A. had strenuously distanced herself from the mother
early, and regarded her as a helpless, useless, denigrated
female with whom she would not want to identify. Later
in her teenage years she had engaged in a sadistic sexual-
ized torture of her brother as a way of getting even with
Mother for taking herself even more out of commission by
giving birth to this hated and embarrassing brother. The
relation with her father seemed exclusive and worshipful.
She gloried in joining his denigration of the mother and
brother. The differences in mental representations for this
patient of the extremely negative adult female, the extremely positive adult male, and the extremely denigrated
child male were canyons apart internally but all significant
(Lax 1997).

Patient B.

This patient, the divorced real estate broker, liked both parents and received much adoration from both of them. They
themselves were animated, humorous and aggressive, much
like my patient, I imagined. They were very distant cousins in a marriage sanctioned to protect the finances. But the
patient felt it was a love match. They frequently had loud
fights, but would as easily make up and be loving and tender again. Ms. B. was convincing and not defensive about
her own amazement that she really had no question about
their love for each other and her in spite of the fights and
storming out of the house to go to the office. They both
pressured little Ms. B. to see herself as the heir to the fam-

ily fortune. "Heir or heiress we don't care" was the essence
of the message. They were sad and disappointed about the
male baby, but readily transferred all of their intense expectations onto their daughter. She was very clever, charm-
ing, precocious, plump, dark, curly-haired, and red-lipped—
good enough to eat, they said, and they ate joyously. There
had been powerful pioneering women in the family in
previous generations and they seemed to feel that a daugh-
ter/heir was entirely adequate. They cared deeply only that
they had a "whiz kid" and interested heir for money management, and they were gratified that Ms. B. was outstanding in math at school, for example, and that she was a class
leader. The mother was a close advisor of the father and
they were "a team" with little Ms. B. as the junior partner.
The image of the boy child, though fearful and negative to
the girl, was also tinged with some tender pathos of the parents' regrets.

A FEW ASPECTS OF THE CONDUCT
IN THE ANALYSES

Patient A.

The young economist headed for the Capitol was fast talking and confident to the point of being obnoxiously full of
herself at times. There was a triumphant air about her,
especially when she had received special comments of praise
from anyone in power. In the transference, she eagerly
sought to find my mistakes, and take me to task for "slop-
py thinking," interferences with her clean lines of logic, and
my interest in her affects. She declared that it was useless
to be angry and worse to know it because it interfered with
"performance." Tears were "revolting" to her and spoiled
her "Look." In essence, unconsciously, she regarded me as a
"wimpy" woman, a caretaker of other "whiny" patients

with whom she abhorred association. Countertransferentially she tapped into some hostility of my own, and protective urges toward my other patients! Her thoughts about my husband were positive. She imagined that he was a brilliant European philosopher and was much in awe of his scholarship. I was portrayed in a dream as a dog with a bandanna around its head, sitting on a park bench. The associations were to a female dog called "Mary." The bandanna reminded her of once tying her brother's wet underpants around his forehead as a punishment for wetting the bed. And the park bench was a symbol of homelessness—a wish, in essence, to kick the bitch and her incontinent son out of the house. I *did* understand the vigorous nature of her oedipal situation but I also thought that Ms. A. was not the nicest person one would want to meet, and sometimes I felt stung by her criticism. She deeply despised women and their birth products.

Patient B.

Ms. B. was rollicking and emotional on the couch. She heaved with fury when she perceived someone being ill-treated. For example, Leona Helmsley, The Queen of Mean, was an anathema image to her. Ms. B. was over generous. For example, she wanted to pay me more than my top fee because she could so clearly afford more and her family thought it a bargain to get analysis in our small city. She wanted to pay more to subsidize poor graduate students she saw in the office suite. We traced her generosity to her profound guilt about being alive when her parents had to suffer through the trials of the baby. She greatly feared that supplies would never truly be enough. They were necessary to salve the inner discomforts of her terror that her own dependent neediness, in conjunction with the guilt that her parents' obvious preference for her had caused the "poor baby's" demise.

BODY IMAGE

Patient A.

I was intrigued from the start with Ms. A.'s "logo" of black with a flash of bright color. I kept relating this picture to the images of her body that were unfolding. The black symbolized sophistication. It was the very opposite of being a baby like her hated little brother. She had a fantasy of being a dominatrix that she had never enacted but had limited to masturbation fantasies. The idea of long black leather boots and tying down a lover excited her. She was always the aggressor. Black seemed the right color to signal control over her environment. The flashes of color represented excitement of one sort or another—"just a hint of the primitive!" she would laugh. "People should beware" when she wore red. "I'm cool, don't touch" was blue. "Keep off the grass" was green. Only yellow was a little vulnerable, a secret sign meaning "I'm scared shitless." I thought that Wilhelm Reich would have had many comments about this patient. Character armor seemed about right for her challenging attitudes. I tried especially to pick "yellow" days to ask about her vulnerable aspects. In response to harsh criticism from men for her aggressivity and sharp tongue, she would toss her head and cope by projecting all the badness to the outside. There was an air of expectation that they would be her victims. She was a conquistador. When I said this she agreed. "Aren't men born to be victims? Even my poor father, married to that hapless bitch." Ms. A. almost had a delusion about how beautiful she was. She thought her beauty made her irresistible to men. Her power over her father and his friends in social circles served to feed these fires of omnipotence. The shape she enjoyed most was the aerobic ideal, with firm lines, minimum curves, and an emphasis on strength. This shape is not only "phallic" but is a specific female androgynous ideal. Ms. A. had been on birth control pills from early on, and clearly viewed control over her periods as quite natural.

It was unclear to me whether Ms. A. had defined any specific gender for herself. She was so much "everything" on the inside and so certain that she could conquer all challenges that it was hard to see any conflict at all. We did sort out why the boyfriends did not last long. They were too ordinary because they expected to be treated as human, with feelings and flesh and blood! Ms. A. did begin to understand that she treated the world in an identical fashion to her notion of home—a place where her father worshipped her power over others; there was no rein on the permission to hurt others; and it was an advantage to hate a traditional female role, citing it as passive and masochistic. I wondered in retrospect if her own unconsciously "monstrous" position in the emotional world was also an enacted version of the inhuman "beast" that she found in her autistic brother. Perhaps my role was to "tame" her by force as she had "tamed" him? We did not complete this analysis, which would have been exceedingly long. We worked for 3½ years before she graduated and left for Washington.

Patient B.

Ms. B. was round, curvaceous, and elegant in her costume. She enjoyed her female habitus in more traditional heterosexual ways than Ms. A. The mother's place on the spectrum of the more to the less traditional, and her place on a spectrum of enjoyment to repulsion played a major role in the favored configuration of these women's female ways in the world. Ms. B.'s bitter and abiding fury at her ex-husband was connected to the fact that he had betrayed her with a young, slim woman and wanted to start another

family. She felt "like a wreck on the sand, washed up, devastated and broken to bits and pieces." She had put on
weight since the divorce, but at the best of times she prided
herself on her large, shapely breasts. She confessed that she
liked to be heavy. It increased her "weight" in the world,
and she also felt respected as a matron. The affair had taken
her by surprise, and in retrospect we thought that she had
always been so much the good, adored daughter that it was
inconceivable to her that someone close could turn away
from her. The husband had led two lives. Ms. B. was wildly
jealous of the younger woman. In analysis, the idea of her
own fierce oedipal jealousy was new. She had suppressed
the jealousy of Mother because she was so caught up in
mirroring and reverberating to the sadness of Mother, being a "good girl" companion to ease Mother's loss of the
"poor baby." She somehow unconsciously expected to be
able to be fully both preoedipal and oedipal without conflict. Ms. B.'s contribution of three grandchildren to her
old parents was another way of making up to them for their
loss. Thus in her female way she played her part in fertil-
izing the seeds of coming generations and in fulfilling their
wishes. It was as if the husband was incidental in the grand
plan for the family millions. It became clear to Ms. B. that
she was so caught up emotionally with her parents that
there was not much room for a husband, beyond the suit-
ability of his "seed money" or genes for the fulfillment of
her encompassing family destiny.

DISCUSSION

These two women obviously were quite unlike each other in
very many ways, as indeed were each of the patients in my
group. Ms. A. was vituperative, vitriolic, and entitled, chilling
in her calculations about how to manage other human beings
to her own advantage. Ms. B. was effusive, warm, and overflow-

ing in emotion and generosity, especially if such emotions complied with an overall scheme of her parents to mushroom and control more and more of their world of finance. One had a sense of Ms. A. as a silver bullet, a powerful family agent of her father. Ms. B. was more likable because she was more developed in her tender relations with others, but she too was a powerful family agent of both her parents, operating like a cloudburst. Each patient was strongly achievement oriented. Each was very gifted and clever. Each was ingenious and creative. Each was healthy and physically attractive. Each was constitutionally highly energetic, dominating, and confident that others would respond positively to them. They enjoyed their aggression more than most—including most men—in my practice. They also pleased themselves first in any interaction with others. With their favored parents there was total accord, so that to please them seemed indistinguishable from pleasing themselves. This form of powerful female is in marked contrast to most case histories in the literature where underachievement, self-effacing qualities, depression, masochism, and guilt are described in overwhelming frequency. At first glance these women would seem to have come from very sad circumstances. It seemed slightly shocking to me to find that such features as lack of empathy or ingrained loathing of their sibling had been so internally rendered that the effects were not nearly as dire as I would have predicted. Perhaps it is an issue of my own judgmental thinking, but I would have thought that girls who had grown up in this way might have had more available tenderness toward their damaged siblings, even in the form of reaction formations. There is a large child psychological research literature on noted symptom and behavior disturbances in the healthy siblings of sick and handicapped children. But Kennedy (1985) states that the healthy siblings of handicapped children are in fact rarely seen by child psychoanalysts. Colonna and Newman (1983) also point to a dearth of in-depth studies of reactions of healthy children to their ill or handicapped siblings.

The child psychoanalytic literature has some reports that seem predictable, for example, accounts of guilty reactions in the healthy children due to their physically favored positions, intensification of sibling rivalry in the healthy children due to overindulgence of the damaged child, or guilt reactions at the death of the damaged child. A dead child is reported to "live on" in response to family wishes and guilts, and the "replacement child" is known to be burdened with the cumulative aspirations of the parents (Cain and Cain 1964). Ms. B. fit the latter category, but the "burden" shared by her bereaved parents, seen from her vantage point as a grown-up, did not ultimately seem all negative. There were pleasurable aspects of being so special to them.

Ms. A., reported here as hard-hearted, surprisingly was more typical of my group in that regard than Ms. B. I assume that Ms. B.'s capacity for feeling tender for and about her sibling had been developed in an embryonic fashion until the relationship was swept away by his death when she was 3. Then her own reaction became complicated within the pathologically rejected mourning reaction of her parents. Empathy for the boy seemed to be virtually absent in cases like Ms. A.'s where the boy was still alive. Often he was institutionalized but she described him bitterly as a burden on the household. I would have expected that the level of unbridled aggression that emerged, exemplified here by Ms. A.'s account of her seductions, would have been combined with evidence of more burdensome conscious or unconscious guilt. Even if remorse was lacking on the surface, I would have expected more embarrassment or shame to accompany the material as they communicated it to me. Elements of pleasurable exhibition seemed more prominent in such accounts. There was a quality of dehumanization toward the damaged brother. In the transference, at those moments in the narrative, I represented the all-approving parent they took for granted, but a parent in fantasy who was collusive with the ill-treatment of the damaged boy. I was supposed to be blind and deaf to the boy, with eyes and heart only for the girl. I was in no way the expectable forbidding maternal or paternal superego imago.

Issues that I have contemplated are such features as the apparent absence of shame and guilt, the nurturance of apparently circumscribed cruelty toward the damaged boy, the boy's role as sadist toward the girl where the boy was older and therefore for a while more physically powerful, the girl's revenge, parental collusion, the sibling's imitation of the parents' relationship, the damaging effects on subsequent relationships as the patients grew up, and pressures and fears of the patients' involvement in procreation and their gender consequences. For example, in these two cases, I naturally looked for signs of guilt at the idea of destroying the boy. Ms. B., the sister of the dead brother, showed guilt. She had the most mature sense of object relatedness in the group. Ms. A. was more typical of others in the group in her lack of guilt. I felt that the stunting of this aspect of her capacity for empathy and her lack of superego reaction to her own aggression resulted from aspects of her identification with and fusion with father in their floridly oedipal father/ daughter bond. As her response to her mother was, in essence, one of disidentification, I believe that this perhaps paralyzed any potential power of the mother's voice in the superego formation.

A NARCISSISTIC WORLD VIEW

I want to emphasize less their individuality in order to enlarge on a few common features of their inner lives that seemed to relate to their success in the material world and their immense ambition. I was in awe of the ego flexibility that enabled them to tolerate large quanta of raw and primitive fantasy, affects (especially aggression), passionate if mainly need-satisfying object relations, and yet enabled them to keep themselves organized in their worlds with good-enough reality testing and affect regulation in spite of elements that might have led one to predict failure. One could as easily draw up a list of intrapsychic vulnerabilities here that would account for a failure to achieve, withdrawal from the environment, borderline functioning with severely disruptive behaviors, impulsivity with markedly self-destructive features, and so on. Yet it is something in the adaptation of these women that I struggle to understand.

As well as this very damaged brother, each woman also had at least one parent who was entirely besotted with and devoted unquestionably to the growing girl's wondrousness and her abilities. The entranced and enthralled parent or parents were also extremely indulgent and lackadaisical about limit-setting. The damaged sibling boys, therefore, had at least one and often two parents who seemed either to despise or want to eliminate them from the family's daily psychological existence—at least as portrayed from the point of view of the psychic reality of my patients. There was a phenomenal contrast in how these parents dealt with the functional girls, my patients, as opposed to their damaged boys.

I believed that all of these patients functioned from within a pregenital psychic world, which they were nevertheless able to adapt sufficiently favorably to match the needs of their outer worlds. They created for themselves environments where their attributes were appreciated and reinforced. I think that their gender identities as externally manifest women aided their advancement in their end-of-the-twentieth-century worlds of business, finance, politics, literature, publishing, and medicine. The women met their social worlds with personal projections of all the positive, all-indulgent reactions that they felt themselves to have experienced with the favored parent. Negatives of any kind, others' reactions, certain affects such as signal shame, sadness, or disappointments, would be met with quick and ferocious anger, keeping "the bad" safely and securely mostly on the outside. Rarely did they find themselves to blame. They quickly restored themselves and, undaunted, they would try again. They could bounce back into the fray, all forces marshaled in record time, appetitive in their desire for mastery. Their desire to "win" was vigorous and highly spirited. Usually they succeeded—at desired jobs, interviews, exams, contracts, positive publicity. "Nothing but the best for me!" said one. "Of course the takeover bid went as planned!" laughed another. "By the way, the movie people want another interview. They loved me!" another said. The amount of acclaim they received from the outside world was remarkable, as it echoed the voice of home from their favored and now internalized parent. They never seemed to tire of either the parental attention or the positive views of outsiders. They hungered for acclaim and often fed luxuriously in fertile pastures. Each had an aura of charisma.

The parents, in their response to the birth of a damaged boy, had communicated their deep and dreadful narcissistic wound and hurt by projecting onto and rendering the child himself as a totally negative creature. This showed in all their ways of representing him to their daughters. It was as if they needed to corral the daughters' hatred of the boy, fueled naturally by ordinary sibling and gender rivalry, to reduce the anxious threat occasioned by any lack of unity on the subject. The sheer physical and mental intactness of the girls became exaggeratedly cherished as utter perfection by them and contrasted with the ruined broken physicality and mentality of the boys. I presumed that the parents must have regressed in their functioning, or perhaps had never themselves progressed beyond life bounded by the passions of all-bad/all-good categories. Many of the damaged children had been sent to institutions. This increased the daughters' sense of having won the competition. Displacing the boy served as a powerful reinforcer to their sense of well-being as the unquestioned favorite. The usual guilt at such a situation seemed to be missing.

Thus by vivid contrast to the bad banished boy, the daughters became all-good. This state of mind was so nurtured that the girl and the parent became one unit, each reinforcing the other while the perceived all-badness of the disappointing boy reduced the threat of imperfection by separating him off. These systems seemed to suggest the power and strength of some of the virtually unassailable and self-satisfied ego ideal of perfection that many of the daughters enjoyed. It was as if the analyst confronted the self-appraisal of not one person but three, all in accord. When Ms. A. quoted her father as saying, "Who is to sit in judgment over us . . . ," I felt that the message was a warning to me, as a representative of the world outside the two of them.

GENDER ISSUES AND OMNIPOTENCE

As the inner world of narcissism prevailed in all of these women, it was accompanied by powerful preferences for fusion and a readiness for symbiotic object relations. Their core gender identities as females were clear to themselves, as is natural. But the later constructions of their gender identities were fluid and interesting creations of blended male and female body aspects and attributes. The subterranean world of omnipotence, as part of the narcissistic developmental realm, is an enchanted place where any fantasy construction can occur. Any body part that is desired for whatever purpose can be adopted into the scheme on a temporary basis and rejected again just as magically, if not successful in creating pleasure by warding off primitive anxiety. The essence of a lack of commitment to either specific gender is the most appealing feature of these patterns.

To use the distinctions suggested by Phyllis Tyson (1982) in considering aspects of the patients' gender construction: Ms. A.'s object choices were first and foremost her father and then other men. In her sexual activity she was vigorously heterosexual. From the physiological standpoint, she enjoyed intercourse, in fact was quite an athlete in bed with her boyfriend

and was multiply orgasmic. She had had many serial boyfriends.
Ms. B. too was heterosexual in her object choice. She had two
children and was divorced. She too had a positive relationship
with her father, and that seemed to influence her choice of male
sexual partners.

As far as gender identity and gender role identifications
went, Ms. B. was mostly identified with the mother in reference to body habitus and her ease in envisioning the function
of her genital organs as integrated in her body image. She echoed her mother's gender role behavior by marrying a man and
producing children. (Her mothering would require too much
space to include here. This was the area of her life in which there
was the most turmoil, especially over battles around independence and the patient's rage at loss of control over the children.)
Her fantasy life and dream life also showed a fascination with
the damaged boy baby as part of her own/mother's body. In
the dreams and thoughts about tumors in her body, she associated with horror not to his penis, which seemed insignificant
compared to his spina bifida, but to his entire body as grotesque
teratomae. These strange lumps she designated as "monsters"
with their haywire growth patterns of hair and teeth. She es-
sentially perceived them as oral and genital horrific part-ob-
jects—invaders of her own body. These pregnancy-type fantasies were also derived from the fantasy of Mother's body
blended with her own. In her dreams she would be impregnated
by Father, and she also impregnated me, giving me
"Rosemary's" baby (also a representation of herself) and her
mother. In fantasy she could fluidly take all roles in procreation
and even take them simultaneously in a single dream. As a pro-
ducer of fantasy, she was at one with her own ideal of possess-
ing the greatest and most productive mental life possible. A
further feature of her mental life was combined male and female images. These represented a fascination with the parents
as a combined and fused unit. Again she could be either or both.
Representations of phallic woman and a simultaneously giant

belly filled with embryos growing bigger and bigger appeared
in dreams. Ms. B. had had three healthy children in her twen-
ties as much needed proof of her genital, inner genital, and body
integrity. These births and her fantasies about them ensured for
her the grandiose family unit. Metaphorically, she was always
in bed with her parents and both outdoing and comforting them
by producing by them and for them. She mentally repeated the
creation of new and improved versions of the damaged infant,
including the fecal infant for all of them. Her fluidity oscillated
readily between dyadic and triadic positions. Money, buildings,
and their acquisition in the material world were thinly disguised
displacements arising from these concerns.

Having unfolded such elements in the analysis, I was surprised by the patient's capacity to fill our sessions with such
primitive material, accompanied by intense fantasy about me
as an archaic parent of either gender, along with her side-by-
side ability to separate successfully from me, get off the couch,
brush herself off as it were, and go into the outside world to
negotiate with others successfully, make her deals, and avidly
engage in corporate finance. I believe that one of her great talents was an access to immense capacities for sublimation.

Ms. A.'s gender identity and gender role identification were
predominantly male and modeled on her favored father, although she too exhibited ongoing fluid creations and re-creations
of bisexually derived fantasy construction. To the extent that
she was proud of her body, dressing it in sleek black, mainly
represented to her an identification with her father's erect adult
phallus. The flashes of color, however, had a different significance. She associated them to feelings (like urine) that she feared
would flow out "too much." One day at the end of a session
she casually mentioned that her brother had a hypospadias. The
horror at his bathroom mess and strange urinary stream seemed
to have become confused for her with all of her affects. I presumed that there must have been much primitive anxiety that
was inaccessible to our analysis and too overwhelming for her

to encounter. The bright colors dotted on her costume actually related to the denigrated boy-penis with holes. This image, of course, was also an omnipotent amalgamation of male and female body part objects. When Ms. A. had intercourse with a man, in fantasy she took away his penis into a hole. She fused with him and together they became one phallus, enjoyably stimulated to ejaculation. Ms. A. was much invigorated by sex with men. She loved the sex act, and her male partners had no complaints. She was not interested in women sexually. The older literature might have considered her necessarily homosexual in orientation. Ms. A.'s simultaneous male part-object body fantasy and yet heterosexual choice of sex partner affirms the theoretical value of separating the object choice aspect from the psychosexual fantasy development of a woman. Ms. A.'s gender role was empowered internally by an incorporation and internalization of her beloved father. The two were in tandem at all times, both in fantasy and in real life. She tolerated what I would have considered as massive erotic overstimulation by him in his desires to accompany her, his intrusive conversations and companionship, just stopping short of overt sex acts. But she really seemed mostly to exult in the idealization and seemed to want this level of involvement. She was amazingly unconflicted about it. I accepted that she was functioning adequately but presumably with marked splits in her ego. I wondered if her sexual cruelty toward Teddy, for example, concealed a helplessness in her relation to her overwhelming father, now expressed as an identification with the aggressor. However, the defense was successful. Her behavior had been in the arena of perversion but had stopped as she grew older. The untroubled nature seemed related to the contemporary powerful fusion with Father and his ego-syntonic denigration of his son. Ms. A.'s relation to her mother in the early years was unfortunately too little known to me. The hatred of females and her thrust to become and be her mother's opposite took over her life and even seemed to energize her strivings. It was not unlike the

disidentification described in a little boy's growth away from
his mother. All the powerful males in her work world were
thinly disguised substitutes for Father, and she used her party
costumes in the female role in order to vamp them.

MEN AS BEAST AND BABY

There is an intriguing double fantasy about men that each of
these women expressed in some form. This "Beast/Baby" fantasy is in form interestingly like the well-known male "Ma-
donna/Whore" fantasy. This double fantasy (traced by Freud
to oedipal dynamics) occurs in the presence of much fear of
women and their power. The Madonna/Whore also represents
an internalized phallocentricity associated with severe denigration of the woman. The Beast/Baby also connotes significant
fear and denigration of the opposite sex. Oedipal dynamics are
one route to this constellation. The fantasized lowly animal
nature of the male is counteracted by imagining his helplessness.
This dual form encodes the male both as boy and adult man.
Mostly the fantasies occur in heterosexual intercourse or masturbation but their derivatives guide daily behaviors. One can
see that it is a version of a little girl's fear, horror of, and excitement about the sexual father, represented as a "Beast." In this
role he violates females to create a monster child (the damaged
brother). In this image he also craves sexual favors from the
woman, who is forced by his wildness to rule him and control
him. His denigrated "animal" desire for sex is his main characteristic.

The boy version is the male as "Baby." Here he is depicted
as weak and helpless, evoking some maternal tenderness that is
laced also with hatred at his weakness and stupidity (reminiscent of the women's attitudes to their disappointing brothers).
Most women in my group were extreme examples of females
in whom worship of adult males disguised great desires to control them through denigration, and for whom images of boy-

maleness held special revulsion and repudiation. Ms. B., even though unsuccessful on the surface in her male relationships, was milder in her attitudes to men than most of the women in the group.

CONCLUSION

These women achieved the kind of power, dominance, and diminishment of the opposite sex that used to be the exclusive realm of men. I wonder if the nether world of parental fusion, narcissism, and gender diffusion actually may have applied to many more men whose power desires and execution would have been taken for granted formerly as merely positive male attributes within the older phallocentric model. The child's psychologically bisexual inner world, environmentally in interaction with male and female adults, allows us to account best for the gendered aspect of sibling rivalries. Body ambivalence, sexual organ ambivalence, and gender ambivalence seem to be the basic building blocks when neither gender is privileged as the template for human development. Using the case of the denigrated boy to test out what can happen to the dynamics of a dominant and favored girl in such a sibship, I suggest that she too can develop the familiar entitled, confident, and arrogant posture, demeaning of the opposite sex and formerly typical of many males in a phallocentric society.

REFERENCES

Balsam, R. H. (1988). On being good: internalized sibling with examples from late adolescent analyses. *Psychoanalytic Inquiry* 8:66–81.

Cain, A., and Cain, B. (1964). On replacing a child. *Journal of the American Academy of Chid and Adolescent Psychiatry* 3:443–456.

Colonna, A., and Newman, L. (1983). The psychoanalytic literature on siblings. *Psychoanalytic Study of the Child* 38:285–309. New Haven, CT: Yale University Press.

Deutsch, H. (1945). *The Psychology of Women*, vol. 2. New York: Grune & Stratton.

Gay, P. (1988). *Freud: A Life for Our Time*. New York: Norton.

Horney, K. (1926). The flight from womanhood: the masculinity complex in women as viewed by men and women. *International Journal of Psycho-Analysis* 7:324-339.

Jacobson, E. (1959). The "exceptions": an elaboration of Freud's character study. *Psychoanalytic Study of the Child* 14:135-155. New York: International Universities Press.

Kennedy, H. (1985). Growing up with a handicapped sibling. *Psychoanalytic Study of the Child* 40:255-274. New Haven, CT: Yale University Press.

Kris, A. (1976). On wanting too much: the "exceptions" revisited. *International Journal of Psycho-Analysis* 57:85-95.

Lax, R. (1997). *Becoming and Being a Woman*. Northvale, NJ: Jason Aronson.

Schafer, R. (1992). Women lost in the maze of power and rage. In *Retelling a Life: Narration and Dialogue in Psychoanalysis*, pp. 128-143. New York: Basic Books.

Solnit, A. (1983). The sibling experience. *Psychoanalytic Study of the Child* 38:281-284. New Haven, CT: Yale University Press.

Tyson, P. (1982). A developmental line of gender identity, gender role, and choice of love object. *Journal of the American Psychoanalytic Association* 30:59-84.

Woolf, V. (1929). (1981) *A Room of One's Own*. New York: Harcourt Brace.`

5

THE LEGACY OF THE DEFECTIVE AND DEAD SIBLING

Discussion of Balsam's Chapter "Sisters and Their Disappointing Brothers"

Harold P. Blum, M.D.

It is a great pleasure to discuss this stimulating, thoughtful, incisive analytic inquiry into a special aspect of sibling relationships. In calling attention to the importance of childhood, psychoanalysis rapidly uncovered the conflictual aspects of sibling relationships and parent–child relationships (Abarbanel 1983, Neubauer 1983, Provence and Solnit 1983, Solnit 1983) Siblings, however, were too often given peripheral consideration in our clinical and developmental literature, and too often that consideration was mainly about jealousy and rivalry.

BACKDROP

Siblings appeared in Freud's own reconstructions such as the birth and death of his little brother, Julius (Blum 1977), and later reconstructions concerning his sisters and his youngest sibling,

his brother, Alexander. This brother's name was chosen by
Freud after Alexander the Great. Freud took his brother on
travels and wrote a paper on their visit to the Acropolis (Freud
1936). Freud was also influenced by his identifications with
Joseph and the sibling figures in the Bible and other literature.
The theory of the superego was foreshadowed in "Totem and
Taboo" (Freud 1913) when Freud proposed that an original
primal horde of brothers developed guilt and remorse after
committing parricide. The case histories all contained references
to siblings, for example, Dora, who was overshadowed by her
brother who was given much more education and who became
the foreign minister of Austria.

The sibling constellations provided by Dr. Balsam are, indeed, a sharp contrast to the typical reports of favored son and
denigrated daughter characteristic of the early literature and, indeed, evident in so many different societies.

Dr. Balsam's chapter intertwines the dual themes of sibling
relationships and female psychology. She rejects the initial patriarchal, phallocentric developmental model in which women
were seen as created deficient. In 1905 Freud wrote that female
psychology was "veiled in an impenetrable obscurity" (p. 151).
A century later the veil has been lifted; many of the early am-
biguities and complexities have been clarified and errors cor-
rected. There is a contemporary emphasis upon a woman's own
attributes—on what she has rather than what she lacks. The
notion of the repudiation of femininity as bedrock (Freud 1937)
is now rarely accepted, as are attempts to derive femininity from
penis envy. In this connection, Dr. Balsam goes beyond
Shakespeare's hypothetical sister and asks what happens in families where the daughter is favored and the son is devalued and
denigrated. She is also careful to indicate that siblings cannot
be considered only in relation to each other but always in relation to their parents and to their parents' relationship to each
other. Her fascinating clinical material actually deals with atypi-
cal sibling situations, in one case a defective or handicapped

much younger brother, and in the other case, the death of a congenitally impaired brother when the patient was 3 and the brother was 5. Dr. Balsam particularly focuses on siblings while trying to explore female psychology. The dual focus is complementary, and yet a complication in her presentation. She asks questions about how the central, unconscious fantasies of these women informed their sexuality, their object relations, their parenting, and their work. The questions stimulate our curiosity, even if we do not have the data for definitive answers or for generalized conclusions.

We need to keep in mind the social structure of the families exemplified by Dr. Balsam's studies and how different the roles and expectations of women are today compared even to the time of the psychoanalytic pioneers and Virginia Woolf. Her patients are not simply nursemaids or housewives; they are talented, ambitious, competitive, successful career women.

DR. BALSAM'S CLINICAL MATERIAL

Let us now consider patient A., the economist who avoided mention of her 12-years-younger brother for months. There was clearly a major familial disturbance after the dysfunctional brother was born. Not only did the brother with pervasive developmental disorder throw tantrums, but the mother and father had screaming fights and could soothe neither each other nor their piercingly, persistently crying son. An inconsolable infant is a painful problem for any family and an urgent reason for medical and psychological intervention. This mother, moreover, had had a difficult pregnancy and was also chronically depressed. This disturbed infant no doubt contributed to an exacerbation of her depression and dysfunction. Divorce among parents of very ill children, such as those with congenital defects or with cancer, is not unusual. The patient was sent to boarding school and, in effect, was divorced from both divorcing parents. Early adolescence was, therefore, characterized by abrupt separation until A. began to become involved with her father, who was particularly charmed by her. One wonders what the arrangements were when she was taken on trips by her father without the security of her mother's presence. Both her infantile narcissistic omnipotence and entitlement and her oedipal conflicts were certainly revived during adolescence. The patient was variously neglected, overindulged, overstimulated, and underprotected. She probably sexually tortured the brother not only out of hatred of him and the mother, as Dr. Balsam suggests, but also enacted her sexual overstimulation by the father with her little brother. Presumably, when she did not talk about the brother, she was identified with the father, who also avoided the brother. The patient had imposed a gag rule on the brother, threatening to cut off his penis. She may have sought transference permission to speak about the unspeakable. The brother was a source of shame and mortification, having cut the patient off from her mother, who probably had never been able to deal with her guilt, grief, and shame concerning her defective child. In addition to the gag rule (a conspiracy of silence), pride and anger defended against conscious shame. Ms. A. may have "belonged in the company of those who designed the planet," far removed from the devalued mother and brother. There was a split between the idealized duo of father and daughter and the devalued duo of mother and brother.

The patient's later exclusive status with her father, with unconscious guilt over her oedipal victory, contributed to the conflict in her relationship with the young man that precipitated her coming in for treatment.

Another split is evident highlighting a limitation of the analytic data and inferences. I refer to the temporal divide, before and after the traumatic birth of the brother. For twelve years this patient was an only child, and a great deal of her personality had been formed before the brother was born. One wonders about the relationship to this chronically depressed mother during the formative years of the girl's childhood. Did she feel guilty about the mother's depression? Did she fantasize that she was to blame or that she and her father would be far better partners, colluding to eliminate the undesirable mother? Her dysfunctional mother is far from a prima donna. She was afraid to identify with her depressed mother or to become like her, and, at the same time, she had to compensate for the mother's defeated hopes. Ms. A. appears to have been secure in her gender identity but unconsciously conflicted about incestuous object choice. She used her close bond with her father to defend against a very early struggle to separate and individuate. Her bond (or bondage) to her father intensified the revived narcissistic and oedipal conflicts of adolescence.

Let us now consider Patient B., the wealthy, divorced woman with three teenage children who had been devastated by her husband's affair and remarriage. A philanthropist, she enjoyed increasing her wealth in both real estate and the stock market. Her parents had rarely talked about her brother with spina bifida and cerebral palsy who died when he was 5 and she was 3. She may have been conceived partly as a fantasied replacement child for the blighted brother. This brother, with severe congenital defects, was the source of pathos and guilt for the survivor patient and her parents. She was clearly the favored child, gifted in math and destined to manage and multiply the family fortune. The parents of a defective child unconsciously wish for the child's death as well as repair and the child's magical transformation into a normal child (Blum 1994). The child may be treated as an object of contempt, shame, and humiliation, a cross to bear, a socioeconomic burden, a scapegoat for other familial and personal problems, a reason for rejection of or reliance upon the partner, a source of masochistic gratification or pride in devotion to the deformed and the handicapped, and so on. The "normal" sibling, while identified with the attitudes of parents and peers toward the defective sibling, is often jealous of the attention given to the sibling's special needs and disdainful of the sibling. There may be denial or reaction formation regarding the reality of the sibling's defects. The mother of a child with Down's syndrome pathetically insisted that everyone she met in the supermarket admire the child.

A child with spina bifida and cerebral palsy usually has varying degrees of difficulty with speech, walking, urinary incontinence, and so on. Other congenital anomalies are common. Such a child may be regarded as a "skeleton in the closet." Spina bifida, now much reduced through folic acid supplements in pregnancy, also has a genetic component. The parents were cousins and may have been carriers, as it were, of a "Rosemary's Baby."

We do not know much about the mothering experienced by Patient B. and by her sibling. Wealthy parents are usually able to assign mothering responsibility to nursemaids and governesses. However, I believe that what needs to be added to the discussion is the likelihood of maternal depression. The birth of a defective child is inevitably a severe narcissistic, depressing blow to the mother (Lax 1972). Patient B. was most likely a great relief to her parents but was also born to a depressed pair into a marriage disturbed by the defective child. Parental fears are realized and hopes are crushed by the birth of a defective child. The child is not looked upon as a gift or narcissistic reward, but as a defective aspect of the self or love object and as a dreadful punishment. As every developmental step is missed or deviant, the parents are continually subject to grief, disappointment, and depression. The onslaught may be particularly severe as the child does not achieve independence and is far more needy than other children whose positive development is a source of parental pride and joy. If the mother of Patient B. was wounded by the brother's death, she was also wounded by the brother's birth and life. The patient and her parents lived with the ghost of the deceased, defective brother. The tormented life of the family around the brother and the patient's subsequent life as an only child may have contributed to her narcissistic demands and expectations.

The family fortune was regarded as a cherished love object, a source of admiration and pride, as contrasted to the feelings about the sibling, who was worthless and shameful. Money management may have rivaled parenting, especially where parenting was associated with narcissistic injury and object loss. That Ms. B. produced normal children was a great solace for her and a gift of grandchildren for her wounded parents. Femininity was associated with injuries, such as her wounded self-image and self-esteem. Did the heiress not have a hidden treasure, a powerful phallus representing the family fortune? As a phallic woman, her bisexuality blended her parents' grand expectations of her being a good mother *and* an aggressively successful replacement of their deceased son. She had the best of both parents while the sibling had their worst.

FURTHER REFLECTIONS

In the case of such severe sibling disorder and death, grandparents may also play a very important role. The depressed mother may be in need of a great deal of psychological support. Fathers, too, have severe reactions to procreating and rearing a defective child. The father, in the case of Down's syndrome to which I referred earlier, became impotent after the birth of his baby. He was inwardly rageful and guilty, determined not to repeat the calamity.

The love/hate relationships between siblings are influenced by identifications with their parents and their common developmental experience. Siblings respond to parental attitudes toward each other and unconsciously to whom the child represents to the parents. The gender of the sibling, the birth order, the age gap between the siblings, and the number of siblings are all important factors. The whole gamut of affective reactions of envy, jealousy, and rivalry on the one side and empathy, sympathy, generosity, and love on the other are strongly influenced by the parents' attitudes and preferences.

The parental attitudes, both conscious and unconscious, as well as the sibling experience, are internalized and often have a powerful influence on standards, values, and ideals. In the case of the women depicted in Dr. Balsam's evocative portrayals, the maternal ego ideal (Blum 1980) may be both excessively vulnerable to regression and dominated by infantile ideals. In the area of parenting, such women may be perfectionists in their demands on themselves as mothers or frightened that their children will be disappointments who will confirm their identification with the depressed mother and the defective siblings. Paradoxically, although favored by their parents, these women have fragile self-esteem. They are identified with their depressed mothers who produced their defective siblings. Survivor victory and guilt is related not only to fantasy but to the reality of sibling impairment and loss. The need for success as mothers and as women in other contexts has a reactive and compensatory function because of their guilt and fragile self-esteem. The defenses against dealing with the constellation surrounding the defective brother and the familial collusive avoidance of discussion and mourning will influence the later analytic work. These patients may need to be successful in analysis while continuing to avoid experiencing the full impact of the sibling transference. The reconstruction of their own tormented, traumatic childhood is vital for analytic progress. Close analysis shows how significant each sibling is to all others and to each of the parents. The wish to be an only child is usually balanced in the only child by a wish for a sibling. Like anatomy, sibling order codetermines destiny. But the attempt to derive major personality features, such as becoming a reactionary or rebel, almost entirely from a single factor like parental preference or birth order (Sulloway 1996) drastically oversimplifies character structure. Sibling relationships may also have an important bearing upon subsequent creativity (Kiell 1983, Pollock 1977), and it is well to remember that concerns for the community, peer relations, and the standard of equal justice for all in part derive from sibling relationships (Freud 1930).

REFERENCES

Abarbanel, J. (1983). Revival of sibling experience in mother's second pregnancy. *Psychoanalytic Study of the Child* 38:353–379. New Haven, CT: Yale University Press.

Blum, H. P. (1977). *Female Psychology: Contemporary Psychoanalytic Views.* New York: International Universities Press.

—— (1980). *Psychoanalytic Explorations of Technique: Discourse on the Theory of Therapy.* New York: International Universities Press.

—— (1994). *Reconstruction in Psychoanalysis: Childhood Revisited and Recreated.* Madison, CT: International Universities Press.

Freud, S. (1905). Three essays on sexuality. *Standard Edition* 7:135–243.

—— (1913). Totem and taboo. *Standard Edition* 13:1–162.

—— (1930). Civilization and its discontents. *Standard Edition* 21:64–145.

—— (1936). A disturbance of memory on the Acropolis. *Standard Edition* 22:239–248.

—— (1937). Analysis terminable and interminable. *Standard Edition* 23:209–253.

Kiell, N. (1983). *Blood Brothers.* New York: International Universities Press.

Lax, R. (1972). Some aspects of the interaction between mother and impaired child: mother's narcissistic trauma. *International Journal of Psycho-Analysis* 53:339–344.

Neubauer, P. B. (1983). The importance of the sibling experience. *Psychoanalytic Study of the Child* 38:325–336. New Haven, CT: Yale University Press.

Pollock, G. H. (1977). The mourning process and creative organizational change. *Journal of the American Psychoanalytic Association* 25:3–17.

—— (1989). *The Mourning-Liberation Process,* vols. 1–2. Madison, CT: International Universities Press.

Provence, S., and Solnit, A. (1983). Sibling experience promoting development. *Psychoanalytic Study of the Child* 38:337–352. New Haven, CT: Yale University Press.

Solnit, A. J. (1983). The sibling experience. *Psychoanalytic Study of the Child* 38:281–284. New Haven, CT: Yale University Press.

Sulloway, F. (1996). *Born to Rebel: Birth Order, Family Dynamics, and Creative Lives.* New York: Pantheon.

6

CHILDHOOD SIBLING RIVALRY AND UNCONSCIOUS WOMB FANTASIES IN ADULTS

Vamık D. Volkan, M.D.

In spite of Freud's recognition that childhood sibling experiences play a role in psychopathology as well as in psychological development (Blum 1977), psychoanalysts have traditionally ignored the role of internalized childhood sibling experiences during the analyses of adult patients. Colonna and Newman (1983) state that "sibling" is not even mentioned in the index of the *Standard Edition* of Freud's collected papers (although Siberia is), nor is "birth of sibling." "Brothers and sisters" and relations between them have just five entries. "Nor do brothers, sisters, or siblings appear in the indices of a large number of general texts on psychoanalysis" (p. 285).

Agger (1988) speculates that Freud's relationships with his own siblings were conflictual and that he might have minimized

Author's note: I wish to thank Michael Houston, M.D., and William Greer, Ph.D., for allowing me to use their clinical material in this chapter.

the role of sibling experiences in the formation of psychopathology because of this. Graham (1988) describes how his own countertransference difficulties interfered at times with his appreciation of the role of sibling representations in his adult patients. He suggests that we should pay more attention to sibling dynamics both in transference and countertransference. He supports his suggestions with clinical material on sibling relationships that emerged from thirty-five psychoanalytic cases.

Like Graham, Sharpe and Rosenblatt (1994) state that the analyst may disregard siblings, not only out of theoretical bias, but because of "countertransference issues related to personal conflicts with siblings" (p. 505). Furthermore, Sharpe and Rosenblatt observe that frequently patients do not mention a crucial sibling even long after parental issues have been significantly explored:

> Some patients, in their intense wish to eliminate their siblings or conflictual feelings about them, have succeeded in lulling us into erroneously thinking they are only children. It is possible that the relative paucity of sibling material in reported cases may result from a narrow analytic focus on ferreting out oedipal and pre-oedipal conflicts with parents. [p. 505]

Sharpe and Rosenblatt conclude that analysts' lack of attention to internalized childhood experiences is an especially puzzling issue since these authors believe that sibling oedipal triangles occur during developmental years. According to them, such triangles exist "independent of parent–child triangles and undergo parallel development into constellations bearing significant formal and dynamic similarities to the standard parent–child oedipal relationships" (p. 491).

Similarly, Graham (1988) reaches the conclusion that there is a distinct line of separation-individuation from early childhood that relates to sibling experiences and that "operates along and/or is intricately linked with infantile attachments to and separations from both parents" (p. 107). Waugaman (1990) describes adult patients who avoid referring to a sibling by name. When they finally disclose the sibling's name, it often coincides with the emergence of sibling-related central conflicts in the transference. Such a disclosure also might accompany associations about an earlier intimacy with the sibling that later gave way to estrangement. Waugaman also notes that in adults' analyses sibling transferences have been largely ignored.

With Ast (Volkan and Ast 1997), I studied the cases of five males and twelve females in which object representations or identifications of childhood siblings played significant roles in psychopathology. We concluded that when childhood representations of siblings and sibling experiences are involved in pathogenic unconscious fantasies, they lead to symptom formations and/or formations of certain character traits. There are many kinds of unconscious fantasies pertaining to sibling images and experiences, such as being a replacement child, being involved in twinning, or forming baby/phallus equations. Among such fantasies, those known as unconscious womb fantasies appear to be most prominent.

UNCONSCIOUS WOMB FANTASIES AND SIBLING RIVALRY

Parens (1980) has described the birth of siblings as an "average expectable event" (p. 419), an event that, although admittedly temporarily disruptive to the psychological equilibrium of the older child, is not necessarily traumatic. If the elder child is being raised in a reasonably healthy environment, equilibrium is gradually reestablished as he or she discovers that there are sufficient maternal resources for both siblings. As older children become more secure in their knowledge and realize that they can share mother with a new sibling without threat to their survival, they begin to relate to their sibling without undue stress. In addition, siblings enhance group feelings and help each other learn a sense of fairness and social justice. We also know of analyzed cases where siblings assumed parental roles toward each other when parenting was not good enough. Be that as it may, the birth of a baby creates for the older child a sudden sense of object loss (Parens 1980). In "normal" situations, this sense of "loss" is worked through and leaves behind only a healthy sense of sibling rivalry.

Sibling rivalry has been observed and written about for thousands of years, so there is nothing new about the phenomenon itself in our modern world. Parents' own unresolved and often unconscious sibling experiences may also influence their children's relationships with siblings. In some individuals, sibling rivalry is maintained throughout childhood and becomes an aspect of adult life. When such an individual enters psychoanalytic treatment, we can examine overt and covert manifestations of sibling rivalry in the patient's behavior patterns, dreams, and transference neurosis. When a patient's symptoms or character traits are rooted in sibling rivalry, focusing on sibling rivalry within the analytic setting may help alleviate such symptoms or modify such traits. In some patients, however, work on the experience of sibling rivalry alone does not lead to improvement since, in these individuals, sibling rivalry does not remain simple and pure but becomes entangled with unconscious fantasies. It is then necessary to reconstruct these unconscious fantasies, bring them into the patient's consciousness, and help the patient work through them within the transference neurosis. One of the key points that separates psychoanalysis proper from psychotherapies, even psychoanalytically informed psychotherapies, is that only in a psychoanalytic setting, and through proper psychoanalytic technique, can successful work be done to render harmless the pathogenic influences of unconscious fantasies.

In 1908, Freud stated that "unconscious phantasies have either been unconscious all along and have been formed in the unconscious; or—as is more often the case—they were once conscious fantasies, day-dreams, and have since been purposely forgotten and have become unconscious through 'repression' " (p. 161). In this chapter, I focus only on unconscious womb fantasies that are related to sibling rivalry. I use the concept of unconscious fantasy in a restricted sense, similar to Freud's second definition, that is, a phenomenon comprised of repressed daydreams, or, more precisely, repressed "interpretations" of a child's experience of a traumatic event. I agree with Moore and Fine (1990) that a description of the unconscious fantasy must incorporate experiences and memories.

Unconscious womb fantasies usually appear in older children who experience their mother's pregnancy as traumatic and the birth of their younger siblings as an intrusion. When these older children undergo psychoanalysis as adults, they often describe previously unconscious womb fantasies connected with sibling rivalries. The story line usually involves the child imagining entering his or her mother's belly and killing the fetus so that he or she will be the sole occupant of the womb. This causes a conflict: the wish to "kill" the fetus clashes with a fear of losing the mother and her love (because she is the carrier of the fetus) or of being punished by the superego. The conflict produces anxiety and the child develops two mental mechanisms that occur simultaneously: displacement and avoidance. The child, or the adult who still has the unconscious fantasy, displaces the mother's womb onto an enclosed space, such as a closet or an airplane, and then avoids being there. In other words, he or she develops symptoms of claustrophobia. There are variations on this theme. Sometimes the patient projects his or her aggression onto the fetus and then is afraid to enter the mother's womb (enclosed space) even while wishing to do so, because on entering it, the patient will face a fetus made ferocious by his or her own projections.

Long ago, Lewin (1935) referred to the unconscious expectation of "meeting" one's father's penis in one's mother's womb as the cause of claustrophobia. Other analysts have reconfirmed this finding. I once analyzed a claustrophobic man who had repeated dreams of swimming comfortably in a warm pool. When in one of his dreams he suddenly found himself face to face with a one-eyed monster in the pool, he woke up full of anxiety. The monster looked like a huge finger pointing up and wearing a hat. Under the hat there appeared one eye. The analysis revealed that this patient's dream expressed his unconscious fantasy of meeting his father's erect penis (the finger) in his mother's womb into which this patient wished to enter. During his developmental years, this patient's mother had kept him dependent on her in a most seductive fashion.

Although Lewin (1935) does not refer to sibling representations in the womb in his examination of claustrophobia, others do (Arlow [1969], for example). Without directly mentioning claustrophobia, Arlow describes how an enclosed space can symbolically stand for a womb. He states that if a patient refers to being in a bus, the analyst should be alerted to the possibility of the patient's reactivating part of a fantasy concerning pregnancy or being within a claustrum. One of Arlow's patients recalled a dream while she was cleaning out a closet, an enclosed space. Her dream concerned being in a diving bell and having an encounter with a shark swimming outside of it. The shark attempted to devour the patient, who was one of a set of identical twins. We can imagine that the shark stood for the patient herself when she expressed rage against her sibling or it stood for her sibling who wanted to intrude into the patient's space. In general, she was preoccupied with impulses of hostility and competition toward her sibling. The analysis of this patient's dream illustrated that "emptying junk out of a closet in reality was in fantasy killing a rival in a claustrum" (p. 17).

In some patients the "enemy" in the womb is both a representation of siblings and of the father's penis. One of my patients, a young woman, would dream of her siblings (appearing symbolically as furry little animals) in her mother's womb, but sometimes a bigger one-eyed creature (father's penis) would appear alongside the sibling symbols.

In addition to producing symptoms, unconscious womb fantasies related to sibling rivalry may also appear in the foundation of character traits. I have treated adult women, for example, who still behave as tomboys, cutting their hair short, climbing mountains, competing with male companions in neighborhood bars or nightclubs by telling dirty jokes, and so on. Yet, beneath such behavior patterns sometimes lies a fear of pregnancy. This fear, often unconscious, is also related to womb fantasies. The wish to kill the fetus inside the mother by exploding the womb may lead to an anxiety of self annihilation since the individual herself also wishes to be inside the womb. This fantasy may change function, mostly due to the patient's identification with her pregnant mother whom she wishes to harm, and may become a fear of pregnancy. The patient may in turn handle this fear by developing unusual tomboyish traits. One such patient of mine would not take the elevator to the third floor of the building where my office was located. At first, she declared that she was an athlete and that walking up stairs helped keep her body skinny (not pregnant). Only much later did she become aware of her anxiety that if she were in the analyst's elevator (womb), her aggression would blow it up, killing her and the other passengers (siblings).

In adults, womb fantasies do not always end up expressing themselves through claustrophobia, fear of pregnancy, or conscious envy and rage toward those who represent childhood sibling representations. Some patients exhibit counterphobic behavior: they compulsively seek to enter certain enclosed spaces that represent the mother's belly. In male adults, the wish to enter the mother's womb repeatedly may sometimes express itself with compulsive heterosexuality. The relationship between unconscious womb fantasies and heightened heterosexuality was first described by Ast and me (Volkan and Ast 1992) when we reported in detail the case of a man in his late fifties who was "addicted to women." He had a long list of girlfriends, and if he could not enter a woman through sexual intercourse he would feel depressed and sometimes paranoid. He made elaborate preparations so that each night he would have a woman. As a child, he had a compulsion to hide in a huge mailbox almost every morning. As a teenager, he was involved in a kind of incestuous relationship with one of his two younger sisters. He would go to her bed and ejaculate over her legs. His analysis revealed that this act was connected with his wish to destroy her, make her a "fallen woman." A nanny in the household had been fired when she became a "fallen woman" (became pregnant out of wedlock). As a teenager, this man was attempting to "fire" his sister from their home.

In my own clinical practice, I never encountered an adult who was the youngest sibling and who had unconscious womb fantasies pertaining to sibling rivalry. Nevertheless, I supervised one case in which this occurred. In this case, the patient's mother was ill when she delivered her last child, and she resented this pregnancy and delivery. The patient's unconscious womb fantasy was mainly a response to his wish to enter his mother's belly to escape her aggression and to have a new "birth." I do not think that this womb fantasy was truly connected with sibling rivalry. It resembled more the fantasies of severely and chronically regressed patients, such as those with severe borderline personality organization. Such patients exhibit unconscious fantasies to be one with their mother by being in their mother's bellies so they can be "reborn."

The rest of this chapter uses three cases to examine the appearance of unconscious womb fantasies connected with older children's sibling rivalry:

1. The first case illustrates how the possibility of the existence of an unconscious womb fantasy can be detected during the diagnostic evaluation and initial phase of analysis.
2. The second case links an unconscious womb fantasy with a peculiar and taboo hypersexuality.

3. The third case examines how an unconscious womb fantasy is brought into transference neurosis and its influence rendered harmless.

Diagnostic Clues about Womb Fantasies

During diagnostic evaluation and initial sessions with our patients, we may begin to determine whether a patient has unconscious womb fantasies related to sibling rivalry and whether they play a role in a patient's psychopathology. When 16-year-old Jack appeared in his analyst's office for the first time, the analyst perceived Jack to be a "sort of large hulking person." Jack was wearing baggy clothes and the analyst could not tell if he was thin or fat, or even male or female. Jack continued to come to his sessions dressed as if he had disappeared under his oversized clothes. During his first session, Jack wanted to explain what was bothering him, and he chose to speak of a problem that had occurred a few hours before he came to see the analyst: at school, the lunch period had been shortened by ten minutes. Jack was upset by this and thought of starting a fire in order to burn the school and the principal.

When Jack's analyst presented this case to me, he had only limited information about his patient, as Jack had been in analysis for only six months. Nevertheless, enough data was available to suggest the existence of an unconscious fantasy that explains Jack's image as someone who was hiding under oversized clothes and Jack's reaction to the deprivation of a full-length lunch period.

Jack has two siblings. The first was born when Jack was 2 years old. It appears that this birth was not unduly traumatic for Jack, but rather an "average expectable event" (Parens 1980, p. 491). Jack's mother's second pregnancy and the birth of his second sibling, a sister, was associated with a fire in Jack's family's apartment and with two separate moves to new locations.

If we consider Jack's story about the lunch hour as a symbolic summary of his intrapsychic problems, or at least an important aspect of them, we may conclude that the external event (fire) which occurred just before the birth of his sister was intertwined in Jack's mind with his aggression. In the story about the school lunch hour, Jack might have been saying that when part of lunchtime (his mother's love) was taken away, his anger could burn his environment (other students/siblings and principal/mother). Taking this a step further, a fire could result in punishment and dislocation for Jack (an eye for an eye).

During the initial six months of his analysis, there were clues to explain why Jack chose to "disappear," not only inside oversized clothes, but also at school where he perceived himself as "a complete zero" compared to other students. When Jack used animal symbols (a typical way of symbolizing children) to refer to his siblings and himself, the siblings appeared as dogs and he appeared as a cat. In reality, his brother and sister had dogs and Jack owned a cat, which had caused an allergic reaction in his brother. At the urging of his parents, the cat was put to sleep—killed—(Jack/cat disappears). Jack told his analyst that the dogs defecated on the family room rug, but that they were not put to sleep. Jack, in turn, would clean the dogs' shit in order to deny his own rage (anal sadism) about his siblings.

Jack spoke of not being an athlete like his brother, in a sense describing how his body symbolically disappeared while his mind flourished: Jack is a poet and reads about psychoanalysis. Another event in Jack's life pertaining to disappearance was directly related to his competition with his sister. Just before starting analysis, Jack learned that his sister was also starting analysis. Unbeknownst to Jack, his parents had decided to finance both children's treatments. When Jack found out, he felt that there was nothing that was just for him. Consequently, he ran away from home; he temporarily disappeared.

Listening to Jack's case, I began to formulate that Jack perceived his second sibling's birth—at the time, he called it "a catastrophe," a big word for a little boy—as an intrusion into his space within his mother's belly. This intrusion led to a feeling of aggression (fire), which burned his mother's belly/apartment. In turn, feeling guilty for wishing his sister dead and for damaging his mother's belly, he unconsciously turned the aggression onto himself while continuing his usual sadistic and cruel behavior toward his sister on a conscious level. His sadism toward his sister, however, was accompanied by the appropriate "submissiveness." Jack spoke of literally eating crumbs left by his siblings when the family ate in restaurants because he was a "nobody."

The act of disappearing has multiple functions for a person like Jack. The guilt punishes him and makes him disappear, but the fantasy may also make him disappear into the mother's womb so that he can be reborn. Baggy, loose clothes may stand for a womb. Also, when he ran away after learning that his sister was starting psychoanalysis, Jack took a bus home. The bus may also represent a womb. I began to formulate that Jack had an unconscious womb fantasy that would read something like this: "In order to please my mother so that she can evolve as a 'good enough' mother, and in order to hide my rage about my siblings, especially my sister, I must disappear into my mother's womb with the hope that I can be reborn and have better parent and sibling experiences."

Initial intuitions and constructions of unconscious fantasies such as the above would of course need to be checked and rechecked. In discussing Jack's case, I simply wish to illustrate how we can hear "clues" pertaining to childhood sibling images and experiences and unconscious womb fantasies during diagnostic evaluation and/or initial phases of treatment.

Taboo Sexuality Related to Unconscious Womb Fantasies

In this case, the existence of unconscious womb fantasies in a 38-year-old psychologist, Steve, was exhibited in sexual activities that would be considered taboo by society and rightly condemned. Intellectually, the patient himself was aware that what he was doing sexually was wrong, but he had a compulsion to do it. When he began his treatment, he was not aware that his sexual involvement with his patients was linked to an unconscious fantasy reflecting his wish to enter his mother's belly and be the only child there. Meanwhile, he was conscious of his ordinary, but intense, sibling rivalry.

Steve's problems started after the birth of his first child, a daughter, seven years prior to his seeking treatment for depression. When he came to treatment, he declared that "everything just seemed to hit the fan" after his daughter was born. "It was then I realized something was missing from the marriage." After this realization, Steve began having affairs with his patients. Two years later, after giving birth to their second child, a son, Steve's wife discovered the affairs, and the couple separated. Meanwhile, one of his patients reported Steve to an investigative board that oversees the practice of psychologists in that region of the country. When Steve came to treatment, he was under investigation by the board.

Steve was the oldest of three children. His two siblings, a brother and a sister, were born two and six years later than he, respectively. His parents, both of whom were college graduates, raised their children in a small, affluent, northeastern town. Steve was somewhat bemused by the fact that although he should have been old enough to remember some of the details of his mother's pregnancy and the birth of his sister, he was unable to do so. Moreover, he was disquieted by his inability to recall anything other than fragmented memories of the birth and early development of his own two children.

Initially, Steve presented an idealized image of his mother, who had died while he was in college, while insisting that his wife, from whom he was separated, was cold and unresponsive to his needs. He repressed the childhood traumas relating to his mother's pregnancies, the births of his siblings, and his mother's erratic behavior when he was young, such as her frequent threats to leave the family, complete with packing of suitcases.

When Steve began his treatment, he spoke of previous treatment with two other psychoanalysts. Later on, there were indications that Steve had dismissed the other psychoanalysts just the way he wished to get rid of his two siblings. There were also other clues pertaining to unconscious aspects of his siblings. Steve related how much he had wanted to be an obstetrician, but at the same time had had fantasies that as an obstetrician there would be occasions when he would not be able to save the lives of babies and their mothers. Babies and mothers could die! Fearing this possibility, he became a psychologist instead.

Steve was aware that when his "taboo" sexual activities started, he felt that his wife loved their children "more than anything else and that perhaps I wished she would love me more than anything else." He ended up having sex with eighteen female patients.

During the first year of Steve's analysis, when his analyst tried to link the birth of Steve's children to his siblings' births, the patient refused to consider such a possibility. Instead, he developed a symptom: he frequently began to call his daughter by his sister's name. This bothered him a great deal, but the symptom continued and eventually led him, with the help of a stronger therapeutic alliance, to consider that his children's births had reactivated in him some repressed aspects of his reactions to his siblings' births. Slowly, his sadistic fantasies regarding his children/siblings began to surface. For example, when he would hear news about hurricanes, he would be terrified about the safety of his children, even if, in reality, they were out of harm's way.

Steve sometimes expressed his fear of "inner city" gangs. After the bombing of the World Trade Center by terrorists, he dreamed of a nuclear explosion that left nothing behind but charred ruins. This dream unrepressed repeated childhood dreams which, Steve believed, were based on a "Superman" television episode. In the recurring childhood dream, parallel to the idea that there were bad guys in the "inner city," there were two bad creatures in the center of the earth. Both the city and the earth stood for his mother's womb, which contained his dangerous rivals. In his recurring childhood dreams, whenever the two creatures escaped from the center of the earth, they frightened him. As a child, when awake, he was afraid of these two escapees. Sometimes he would imagine them to be under his bed. He would put toy battleships around his bed to protect himself from these creatures that, as he slowly began to understand, had represented his sibling images. The dangerous nature of these sibling images was magnified because of Steve's projections of his own aggression and murderous rage onto them.

Detailed stories of his affairs with female patients shed further light on his unconscious fantasies. Steve himself would regress with his female patients, obviously not in the service of helping these patients, but in the service of his neurosis. His psychopathology was connected with his wish to be the only one in his mother's belly. He would either choose childless women or mothers whom he perceived as rejecting their own children while adoring him.

Once, while his wife was away and he was looking after the children, Steve took one of his patients to his wife's home and *chose* the children's bedroom, where they lay sleeping, to make love to the woman. As the house had other available rooms, it was an irrational act, but he had a compulsion to do it. In this enclosed space where both children slept, he wanted to be sure that a symbolic mother would please only him, that he was the only one entering her vagina/belly. His taboo hypersexuality had elements that related to his taboo incestuous, oedipal wishes. But, as Steve's associations indicated, the main meaning of his hypersexuality lay in the service of gaining entry into and sole occupancy of his mother's belly, thereby allowing him to win the competition with his siblings/children.

It is beyond the scope of this chapter to give details of Steve's treatment except to indicate that during his sessions, again and again, his associations would turn to his siblings/children. On one occasion, for example, he described a rationalization for canceling his son's birthday party, which was an expression of his wish that his children/siblings had never been born.

Steve also competed with his analyst whenever he perceived the analyst as a sibling. Nevertheless, during the initial years of his analysis, he was not deeply involved in taking responsibility for and working on the new material that was now available to him. In other words, during the first two years of his treatment, Steve did not evolve a true transference neurosis. The main reason for this, besides his unconscious competition with his analyst/sibling, was due to the investigation that hung over his head like the sword of Damocles. It was an "external superego" constantly punishing him. During these initial years, Steve was carrying on an affair with a woman who had two children, but who behaved, in Steve's mind, as if she did not care for them, but loved Steve more. Meanwhile, as his wife remained preoccupied with the couple's children, with whom Steve competed in an overt fashion, he perpetuated the image of his wife as ungiving.

When the investigative board finally reached a decision, it was milder than Steve had expected. The sword of Damocles was removed. With this development, Steve developed an intense transference neurosis in which he perceived his analyst as a severe superego. He was also concerned with intruders (the analyst's other patients). Slowly, the connection between his desire for punishment and his desire to "kill" his siblings and occupy his mother's belly (the analyst's office) surfaced. At the present time, Steve's analysis continues, and he is working on his problems.

The Appearance of Womb Fantasies in Transference Neurosis

Unconscious womb fantasies related to sibling rivalry may be constructed during analysis and intellectually accepted by a patient. Nevertheless, rendering their influence harmless occurs only when such fantasies are included in "therapeutic stories" (Volkan 1984). The therapeutic story is a specific type of transference neurosis: the patient creates a story that is not simply reported, but rather lived by the patient. In a sense, the unconscious fantasy comes to life as if the patient were the writer, director, and actor in a play. The patient's actions do not fit the description of what is known as acting out, but are in the service of sustaining the story, which progresses over many sessions and which comes to an end when the patient tames the affects pertaining to it. The analyst, representing various transference figures, is also included in the therapeutic story.

Therapeutic stories are experienced by the patient as more real than typical transference distortions. Since unconscious fantasies are real in the patient's mind, mere construction of them in sentences and interpretation of their function may not be enough to render their influence harmless. A mental reality in the unconscious has to be matched with a transference reality so that the patient, after working through the conflicts within the therapeutic story, frees himself or herself from clinging to the unconscious fantasy. In this fashion, the unconscious fantasy may be neutralized, though I believe it can never be totally removed.

In our book on siblings in the unconscious, Ast and I (Volkan and Ast 1997) describe in great detail the case of Lisa, a college student whom I analyzed. Though many aspects of her case are fascinating, I will limit my discussion here to the story of bringing her unconscious womb fantasy to transference neurosis.

Lisa exhibited the most typical womb fantasy related to sibling rivalry. She wanted to enter her mother's belly, kill her two younger brothers, whom she considered "intruders," and be the only occupant of her mother's womb. In the third year of her analysis, after she and I had reconstructed her unconscious fantasy, and after she had done a great deal of work on understanding its influence on her, Lisa declared that she had found employment as a waitress in a restaurant. At first, the importance of this information escaped me. Little by little, she informed me that this restaurant was in a basement and that one had to go down a narrow "tunnel" to enter it. I thought that it symbolically represented her mother's womb since, in the past, Lisa had utilized similar locations as womb symbols. Lisa said that she was not ready to tell me the name of the restaurant or its location. Such information should be her secret. "If you know which restaurant I work at, you will come in, and if you do, I will melt. I'll be liquid. You are Mafia. If you come in, you'll shoot me. You don't know, but I have been living in anxiety for months that one day you would walk into this restaurant. You will come in and *bug* me, torment me." The reference to my "bugging" her was especially interesting, as Freud (1900) noted that often in dreams siblings appear as bugs.

At this point, I knew that a therapeutic story was evolving and, as the restaurant was going to be Lisa's mother's womb, I was going to represent her siblings. One of the most important technical maneuvers is not to interfere with the evolution of the therapeutic story by premature interpretations or endless conversations with the patient.

Now Lisa's sessions centered on the reality of her therapeutic story. She would come in, lie on the couch, and right away continue with reports on her involvement with the restaurant as if nothing else mattered. Sitting behind her, I was beaming with pleasure at her ability to bring her unconscious fantasy into "reality." As I sat silently, she screamed at me: "I don't want you to come in. If you come in, I'll throw you out; I'll kill you!"

Once, she described how she would go to the restaurant's kitchen area and sharpen knives in the event I entered the restaurant. She would watch the street from a small basement window through which she could see people's shoes as they walked by the restaurant. Once she thought she recognized my shoes and became anxious.

During Thanksgiving break, when she was separated from me, my image in her mind changed and became her mother's image. I learned through her report of a dream that she decided to be in her mother's womb and thus not separated from me/mother. In the dream, she found herself in an enclosed space: "I was inside, way inside," she said. "The walls were pink, soft, and puffy, like cotton." She associated this with her fantasy of being in a womb.

One day Lisa heard a crying child at the store where she was shopping and immediately thought of her dream. Suddenly, she recalled that as a child she had felt extremely hurt and had cried herself to exhaustion when her brothers' births and her mother's postpartum depressions had caused her intolerable trauma.

After Thanksgiving, she said that being in a womb no longer satisfied her. She reported a dream that reflected her wish to be outside her mother's belly. She said that in the new dream, a woman who looked like a reptile swam out of dark waters to the shore where there was sunshine. "The reptile was me," Lisa said. "I felt good, but if I am outside the womb, they'll know I am not a nice little girl. I am angry!"

Lisa began reading about the concept of territoriality in the animal kingdom and dreaming about rats (her brothers) in the restaurant-like place. In one dream, the baby rats were wearing Virginia Military Institute uniforms. It should be recalled that first-year cadets at that institution were called "brothers rat" at that time. It was difficult for Lisa to tolerate the rats; they made her anxious. Eventually the rat dreams ended as Lisa learned that territoriality in some animals served to maintain borders around territories so that they would not kill each other. The last rat dream reflected a significant change in the dream's story. Lisa said: "I saw my brothers in the womb. They were not scary anymore. The rats were newly born with no fur; they were just pink. I could look at them and accept them without anxiety." It was then that Lisa told me the name of the restaurant. Her therapeutic story had lasted about three months.

CONCLUSION

Unconscious womb fantasies related to sibling rivalry may remain influential in the minds of adults and be crucial in the development of psychopathology. Such psychopathology may express itself with symptom formations (i.e., claustrophobia or compulsive seeking of enclosed spaces) or character traits (i.e., a woman behaving like a man as a habitual defense against pregnancy). I have described the diagnosis of several manifestations of such sibling-related unconscious fantasies in the clinical setting and reported how their influence can diminish when patients reactivate them in "therapeutic stories" and work through the associated conflicts.

REFERENCES

Agger, E. M. (1988). Psychoanalytic perspectives on sibling relationships. *Psychoanalytic Inquiry* 8:3–30.

Arlow, J. (1969). Unconscious fantasy and disturbances of conscious experience. *Psychoanalytic Quarterly* 38:1–27.

Blum, H. P. (1977). The prototype of preoedipal reconstruction. *Journal of the American Psychoanalytic Association* 25:757–785.

Colonna, A. B., and Newman, L. M. (1983). The psychoanalytic literature on siblings. *Psychoanalytic Study of the Child* 38:285–309. New Haven, CT: Yale University Press.

Freud, S. (1900). The interpretation of dreams. *Standard Edition* 4, 5.

——— (1908). On the sexual theories of children. *Standard Edition* 9:205–226.

Graham, I. (1988). The sibling object and its transferences: alternate organizer of the middle field. *Psychoanalytic Inquiry* 8:88–107.

Lewin, B. D. (1935). Claustrophobia. *Psychoanalytic Quarterly* 4:227–233.

Moore, B. E., and Fine, B. D. (1990). *Psychoanalytic Terms and Concepts.* New Haven, CT: American Psychoanalytic Association and Yale University Press.

Parens, H. (1980). Psychic development during the second and third years of life. In *Course of Life*, vol. 1, ed. S. I. Greenspan and G. H. Pollock, pp. 459–500. Bethesda, MD: NIMH.

Sharpe, S. A., and Rosenblatt, A. D. (1994). Oedipal sibling triangles. *Journal of the American Psychoanalytic Association* 42:491–523.

Volkan, V. D. (1984). *What Do You Get When You Cross a Dandelion with a Rose? The True Story of a Psychoanalysis.* New York: Jason Aronson.

Volkan, V. D., and Ast, G. (1992). *Eine Borderline Therapie.* Göttingen, Germany: Vandenhoeck & Ruprecht.

—— (1997). *Siblings in the Unconscious and Psychopathology.* Madison, CT: International Universities Press.

Waugaman, R. M. (1990). On patients' disclosure of parents' and siblings' names during treatment. *Journal of the American Psychoanalytic Association* 38:167–194.

7

SIBLING RIVALRY: A PHENOMENON OF CONSTRUCTION AND DESTRUCTION

Discussion of Volkan's Chapter "Childhood Sibling Rivalry and Unconscious Womb Fantasies in Adults"

Barbara Shapiro, M.D.

Dr. Volkan thoughtfully describes some of the ways in which normal, average, and expectable human feelings of sibling rivalry can take on malignant properties, transformed into hatred, overwhelming jealousy, spiteful envy, omnipotent possession, and unmitigated contempt. He points out the clinical and theoretical lacunae that occur when psychoanalysts consider parents but not siblings. His discussion illustrates the genetic and developmental significance of sibling rivalry as an entity in its own right. To this end, he focuses in general on pathologic sibling-derived material and in particular certain unconscious womb fantasies. This focus is necessary for heuristic purposes. However, just as Winnicott's baby cannot be understood without a mother—although we certainly can discuss the baby and the mother separately—so also the developmental course of sibling rivalry and the resulting endopsychic representations cannot be understood without considering the parents and the family.

Also, the sheer "noisiness" (Kris and Ritvo 1983) of malignant rivalry may eclipse the more quiet ways in which sibling rivalry contributes to adaptation. In this discussion I would like to put womb fantasies and sibling rivalries into a larger context: the family cradle-crucible.

OEDIPUS AND SIBLINGS

The Oedipus legend is an illustration of the crucible within which destructive object relations with both parents and siblings are forged. We tend to think of the Oedipus legend as pertaining to children and parents, and not to siblings. Freud saw the relevance of the analysis of the psyche, as contained within literature and myth, for his clinical observations, and masterfully integrated these spheres. The significance of his synthesis of literature and observation can be extended, as the Oedipus saga powerfully depicts hostility and destructiveness in sibling relationships. As my source, I use Sophocles' version of the Oedipus legend as found in his Theban plays: *Oedipus Rex* (442 BC), *Oedipus at Colonus* (435 BC), and *Antigone* (446 BC).

Oedipus and his wife-mother Jocasta had four children—two boys, Polyneices and Eteocles, and two girls, Antigone and Ismene. After Oedipus discovers that he has murdered his father and married his mother, without conscious intent, he blinds himself and becomes a wandering outcast. His daughter Antigone accompanies him and attends to his needs as a nonsexual mother-wife. Antigone's sister Ismene plays a lesser role in the triangle of father and two daughters. Meanwhile the two brothers fiercely battle over which one is to rule the city. Eteocles, the younger, defeats his older brother Polyneices. The older furiously plots to regain power. Oedipus, in a fit of fury, renounces both his sons and dies. The two brothers then murder each other. The story gets more complicated. Creon, the brother of Jocasta and now the king, decrees that Polyneices is to be denied a proper burial by the state. Since this means that he will never be with the gods, his sister Antigone, who loves her brother as she did their father, Oedipus, decides she will bury her brother's corpse, knowing that if she does so she herself will be executed for this act of treason. She asks Ismene for help, but Ismene declines, saying that the act is futile. Antigone hates her sister for this perceived betrayal, even though what she asked of her would surely result in death for both. In a heated exchange between the two sisters, Antigone dismisses Ismene: "if now you wished to act, you wouldn't please me as a partner." Ismene, however, proclaims love for Antigone, and urges her to at least bury Polyneices secretly, to avoid execution by the state. Ismene then vows her own silence to protect her sister. Antigone erupts with fury. "Dear God! Denounce me. I shall hate you more if silent. . . ." Antigone buries Polyneices and is condemned to death by Creon, despite the fact that his own son loves Antigone and pleads with his father for his beloved's life. Here the father effectively murders his son (who kills himself after Antigone's death). After Antigone's burial of Polyneices is publicly exposed, Ismene offers to share responsibility for the act, knowing that she too will be executed, but with her sister. Antigone bars her from this, saying, "I cannot love a friend whose love is words." Ismene pleads, "Sister, I pray, don't fence me out from honor. . . ." We start to wonder if Ismene is motivated by guilt and shame rather than by love for her sister, and whether protestations of love disguise cowardice at the loss of honor. Antigone hates her sister for first not helping her and then having the nerve to try to claim some of the responsibility for what was Antigone's act. Antigone declares, "Don't . . . make your own that which you did not do." Ismene sees her sister's hatred and says, "Why hurt me, when it does yourself no good?" Antigone's reply shows that the victory of sibling estrangement brings no peace. She says, "I also suffer, when I laugh at you." Ismene ends up killing herself, as does just about everyone else.

I think most of us would agree that Oedipus' family is riddled with problems, multifaceted and spanning several generations. The parents of Oedipus, Jocasta and Laius, try to bypass fate by piercing their own baby son's ankles with thongs, binding his legs, and telling a servant to "make away with him." Oedipus himself is abused and abandoned. This dooms him to the unconscious fate of murdering the father and marrying the mother of whom he had no conscious awareness. We see ghosts of the past as Antigone sacrifices herself for her father and then for her brother (Lacan 1959–1960). Antigone speaks of her own soul murder: "My life died long ago" (Vestin 1997). It is within this family context of multigenerational trauma, denial, and unconscious oedipal victories within shifting triangles of siblings and parents that sibling rivalry and conflicts of ambivalence are forged into hatred, murder, and suicide. Malignant sibling hatred and destructive repetitions of the past do not spring up in a vacuum. Yet this tragedy illustrates that no one person or generation is to blame. Who is responsible for "fate," a word I might translate into the vicissitudes of development when unconscious fantasies, conflicts, and self and object role representations are hidden, denied, or split off, as happened to baby Oedipus. His parents attempted to deny his very existence. Yet even their actions can be understood as trying to escape a terrible fate for themselves and for their son.

SIBLING RIVALRY:
THE DEVELOPMENTAL COURSE

Dr. Volkan describes how sibling relationships may be intertwined with developmental and conflictual impasses. His descriptions are in accord with other reports in the literature (Bank and Kahn 1982, Shapiro et al. 1976, Sharpe and Rosenblatt 1994). We do not always encounter the extremes of sibling murder and suicide described by Sophocles. However, we all see patients with similar conflicts, usually, although unfortunately not always, on a smaller scale. A key question is: What keeps normal and expected sibling rivalry from becoming structured into malignant hatred?

Dr. Volkan describes three patients, all of whom are oldest children, with the younger siblings born during the first six years of their lives. Some authors have proposed schemata for understanding the effects of birth order (Sulloway 1996). Such formulaic descriptions ignore the complex, overdetermined, and multifaceted ways in which any event becomes woven into psychic structure (Agger 1997). However, without making reductionistic predictions, we can examine how sibling relationships develop for older and younger siblings.

Freud (1900) commented on older and younger siblings in *The Interpretation of Dreams*. "The elder child ill-treats the younger, maligns him and robs him of his toys; while the younger is consumed with impotent rage against the elder, envies and fears him, or meets his oppressor with the first stirrings of a love of liberty and a sense of justice" (p. 202).

Provence and Solnit (1983) and Parens (1988) describe observational sequences of sibling relationships. For older siblings the baby is a new object, and has not always been present. As such, the baby intrudes on preexisting relationship patterns. The quality and content of the intrusion and potential rivalry are influenced by many factors, such as the older child's age and psychic structure, the family dynamics and structure, and external events and stressors. However, we can say that in general children, especially those who have not yet adequately resolved separation, individuation, and oedipal issues (either due to age or due to developmental variations or impasses), usually regard the new baby as an intruder, a rival.

Conversely, for the younger child, the older sibling has always been present (Provence and Solnit 1983). Thus, by definition, the older child is not initially an intruder and becomes a rival in the younger one's eyes only after some differentiation of self and other has been achieved. Sometime during the middle of the first year babies respond to their older siblings as objects of attachment, cooing, smiling, and reaching out their arms when the older sibling enters the room (Parens 1988). With the development of locomotion, the baby takes the older sibling's toys, much to the exasperation of the sibling. In part the taking of the toys is exploration: the love affair with the world. However, Parens also describes the phenomenon of "wanting what the other kid has" developing toward the end of the first year of life (Parens, this volume). This phenomenon does not go away. We often see ourselves and others wanting what the other person has. We hope, however, that this wanting will undergo ego modification and sublimation, rather than evolve into destructive envy and compensatory entitlement.

An example of the interaction of rivalry and "wanting what the other kid has" is contained in the following clinical vignette:

A 15-year-old patient was musing in her analytic session about her relationship with her sister, five years older. She described her living room. "We have a three-seater sofa and a chair, and there are four of us. I have always been the one who has to sit in the middle. The better seats are on the outside of the sofa—that way you get more room and the arm of the sofa—or on the chair, but the chair belongs to my father. The person in the middle gets squished, but that's what happens when you're the little sister. I always get the middle and my sister gets an arm. But now my sister wants the middle, and I don't want her to have it. It's my place and I'm used to it—and anyway in the middle I can be close to people even if I am squished. Why does she want to take my place? It's my space, my territory. It's not as good as she has, and she wants it."

By the second year the squabbles start, and the younger child more and more actively competes with the older for things as well as for the parents' time, attention, affection, and preference.

As the self develops and becomes differentiated from the object (often marked by the toddler's declaring that everything is "mine"), rivalry becomes more intense, and we begin to see differential development of rivalry, envy, and jealousy (Neubauer 1982, 1983). However, this is often mixed with adoration, imitation, and wanting to be like the older sibling. The older child usually does not view the younger child in this way (Neubauer 1983).

SIBLING RIVALRY AND ADAPTATION

The arrival of a new baby and sibling rivalry are normal and expected events in the lives of children (Bank and Kahn 1982, Hartmann 1939, Parens 1988). However, average and expected events are not necessarily easy. In reality the presence of a new baby usually means less time for the older child. (Kris and Ritvo 1983) The parents are tired, deprived of sleep, and preoccupied. Given this reality, we can wonder why sibling rivalry does not usually become malignant. I would like to discuss four modifiers of sibling rivalry for the older child: (1) the adequacy of libidinal supplies, (2) parental love for all the children, (3) continuing parental relationships, and (4) the attachment of the baby for the older sibling.

The Adequacy of Libidinal Supplies

First let us consider the adequacy of libidinal supplies for all members of the family. The birth of a child represents a nodal point, a potential crisis, in adult development. As with most nodal points, some regression is necessary to promote progression. Inherent in the mother's ability to mother is regression in the service of bearing and nurturing a baby (Kestenberg 1976). In this process the mother herself needs a mother. If a father is present, he (it is hoped) fills that role. Alternatively, other family members, friends, community supports, or groups (such as new mothers' groups) may support and nurture the mother. A removed or detached father is not only of no help to an overwhelmed mother, but may actually interfere with the possibility of obtaining help through other spheres. For example, friends and community supports are more readily available for single mothers than for depressed mothers in apparently intact families. Sometimes no resources are available. In that case, if the inner world of the mother is exceptionally rich in libidinal supplies, she may be able to care adequately for herself, the baby, and any older children. This process would be similar to the resilient child capable of extracting libido from impoverished sources (Mahler et al. 1975). However, one expects that most mothers require adequate external libidinal supports. These external supports act as a psychosomatic selfobject—psychosomatic because intrapsychic workings are reflected in somatic processes during pregnancy, childbirth, and care of the baby. For example, Kennell and his co-workers (1991) documented that the presence of a support person during labor decreased both the length of the labor and the complications. Child bearing and child care inherently involve both the psyche and the soma.

Additionally, the mother must be psychically able to accept and benefit from external libidinal supplies. Maternal depression, internal conflicts, or overwhelming external stressors may preclude the ability to take in, and thus to give. In at least two of the three cases cited by Volkan, the mothers were depressed and the fathers unavailable.

When libidinal supplies are adequate, and if other problems do not interfere, parents can tolerate the older child's usual regression without belittlement, while at the same time reinforcing to the child that she has wonderful abilities that the baby does not. Thus the child can regress and progress at the same time, without either action risking actual loss of the object or the object's love. The child can reexperience being a baby as she watches the baby—a regression of sorts—and at the same time progress as the parents tell stories about "when you were a baby" (Provence and Solnit 1983). In this way regressive identification is put into words, enabling mastery and ego growth.

In contrast, regressed and depleted parents may project their own self hatred onto the child when the child regresses.

Parental Love for All the Children

The older child must see that the parents are able to love the new baby while continuing to love the older child despite her entreaties to "send it back" or some other such variation. An attuned and nondepleted parent responds to the child's fervent wishes for the baby's disappearance or demise with empathy (Kris and Ritvo 1983). Such empathy is not possible if the new baby is unwanted or hated by the parents, consciously or unconsciously, or if the new mother is significantly depressed. When the child sees that her wishes for the baby's destruction are not actualized, the push toward the reality principle and away from omnipotence is reinforced. The child is less likely to become terrified of her own aggression (Provence and Solnit 1983), which in turn reinforces object constancy and the growing ability to distinguish reality from fantasy, thought from deed. The demonstration that libidinal supplies are ample and can be shared without being diminished provides a lesson in the nature of love, allowing the child to free her love objects to pursuits of their own. Obviously, if libidinal supplies are not adequate, external reality reinforces fears of loss of the object and of the object's love. Rivalry then is rooted in reality and becomes entrenched. When the parents visibly love the baby, the child can also begin to love the baby in identification with the parents. All this assumes that the older sibling is not excluded or ignored, and that the parents keep the younger child from intruding into the older one's territory.

Continuing Parental Relationships

If the family consists of two parents, the child ideally sees that the parents continue their relationship. This balances oedipal fantasies that the baby is the child's own, or that the child's murderous and incestuous wishes have been actualized. The child can be aware of her own wish to have a baby (Parens 1988) without the danger of a fantasied oedipal victory becoming too real.

Attachment of the Baby for the Older Sibling

As the baby grows and begins to smile and respond to the older sibling, cooing and reaching out her arms when the older child enters the room, the older child begins to feel herself as the object of love and can respond in kind. Feeling loved is a powerful inducement to love. Also, the older child's sense of mastery is augmented as she has the opportunity to act as an auxiliary ego for the younger (Parens 1988). Here parental reactions are important. A jealous or hostile parent may not encourage sibling love, and a depleted parent may overuse the older child as a substitute parent.

Even the most optimal environment coupled with the most temperamentally mellow child does not prevent rivalry, jealousy, and envy, nor would we wish it to do so. These emotions are part of the substrate of our everyday lives as adults if we live in proximity to others and not in isolation. We can see the adaptive force of rivalry by examining the derivation of the word. The word *rival* comes from the Latin *rivalis*, meaning "one living near or using the same stream as another" (Neubauer 1982, Webster 1962). Rivalrous struggles force proximity and block isolation. Isolation occurs only when a child retreats from the fray. As children we can learn major ego functions such as mutual cooperation, coordination, and sharing, so that everyone has access to clean water. Alternatively we can pollute the water, block access, or engage in open warfare. Obviously, if the water supply is inadequate or already contaminated, rivalry becomes a fight for either one or the other to survive.

For both the older and younger child, rivalry provides a powerful push toward separation and individuation (Abelin 1971) if it is not forced into destructive aggression or crystallized into rigid hatred. For example, with the birth of a new baby, frequently the father or his substitute becomes closer to the older child, taking her for walks, providing daily care, discussing difficulties, and so forth. Such activities, with the resulting closeness, help with separation from the mother (Mahler et al. 1975), and take advantage of the potentially maturing aspects of a developmental nodal point. Kernberg (Kernberg and Richards 1988) cites the example of Little Hans. In an example of what in modern times we might call male bonding, Hans's father was the one to seek the counsel of another man, Professor Freud, to help his troubled son. Little Hans's problems were not just derived from classic oedipal struggles. Hans was 3½ years old when his sister was born. At the time of Freud's intervention, Hans "frankly confessed to a wish that his mother might drop the baby into the bath so that she would die" (Freud 1900, p 203). The process of drawing closer to others in order to separate from the mother and tolerate the new baby can also occur among siblings. An older sibling may band with or even nurture a slightly younger sibling, providing support for coping with the intrusion of the baby (Leichtman 1985). When the developmental space is closer, there may be more synchrony of interests (Solnit 1983). Conversely, with wide age ranges, the older sibling is more likely to act as a parent. Sibling bonds and support are unique and may be of particular help, as children often find each other more understandable than do the adults in their lives (Agger 1988, Provence and Solnit 1983). Overall, rivalry, envy, and jealousy force children to seek differences and niches, while engaging in an intimate rough and tumble with others of their own size. The intimacy and aggression together provide force for identifications, while the awareness of differences coalesces self identity.

At the same time, recurring humiliating sibling defeats can cause severe narcissistic blows. Rivalry exists with both parents and siblings. However, competitive losses with the same-sex parent can be tempered by the difference in generations, assuming good-enough parenting and an adequate fit between parent and child. The child is consoled that one day she too will be an adult and be able to do grown-up activities, but right now she is actually little and inexperienced. In the rivalry between siblings, particularly those close in age, there is no consolation prize for repeated losses or sustained experiences of inadequacy (Sharpe and Rosenblatt 1994), except by finding another arena for competition and success.

DISCUSSION OF CASES

The Case of Jack: The Metaphors of the Analyst

The first case, Jack, is a 16-year-old poet who reads about psychoanalysis while making his body disappear under baggy and formless clothes. Dr. Volkan hears this as a possible "womb fantasy." Obviously, as Dr. Volkan points out, there are many possible explanations for Jack's appearance and symptoms. To me Jack sounds like an intellectually precocious youngster with a libidinal cathexis of the mind, and a denial, dismissal, turning away from the body. Winnicott (1988) describes this process as the *mind-psyche*, where "the mind . . . has a false function and a life of its own, and it dominates the psyche-soma instead of being a special function of the psyche-soma" (p. 140). Perhaps these are two different but equally valid metaphors or paradigms to explain the same phenomenon. I speak here of how the irreducible subjectivity of the analyst, including her or his favorite metaphors and theories, inevitably influences the way material is heard, understood, and interpreted, and in turn the manner in which the analysis unfolds.

The Case of Steve: Boundary Violations, Ghosts, Siblings, and the Superego

Steve, the psychologist, was haunted by hateful intrapsychic representations of his younger sister. As a mental health professional, I read with horror that the professional board made a "relatively mild" decision for this psychologist who slept with eighteen of his female patients. Of course I do not know what "relatively mild" means. I would hope that the flagrant and repeated boundary violations would prompt the removal of Steve's license to practice.

Whatever the actions of this particular professional board, we know that all too often significant boundary violations elude adequate professional intervention. Obviously this is a multifaceted phenomenon. However, dynamics in professional groups often partake of aspects of sibling relationships, including conflicts of loyalty and betrayal. We are all familiar with the situation in which we allow ourselves to criticize our own siblings, but woe befall the outsider who ventures the same observations. Especially in difficult circumstances, groups of siblings or sibling substitutes can band together very powerfully, providing mutual protection and support. One dramatic example is the group of children described by Anna Freud—the orphans of Terezin—who grew up together in the concentration camps without caring adults. These children loved one another, hated and distrusted outsiders, and rarely squabbled (A. Freud and Dann 1951). Such sibling protection, however, is often not the case. In the absence of a parental base, siblings may not be able to integrate at all (Solnit 1983). They may isolate themselves from one another, and/or engage in fierce warfare. The rivalrous struggles can become physically and verbally abusive.

Sibling love is only one force underlying sibling loyalty, although certainly a most important one. Siblings are usually acutely aware of one another's crimes and misdemeanors, especially if they are close in age. They have the ability to unmask each other, to get the other sibling into trouble with the older generation if they choose to do so (Bank and Kahn 1982). In *King Lear*, Cordelia says to her sisters, "I know what you are, and like a sister am most loath to call your faults as they are named" (Shakespeare 1594, I:2). Often there is an implicit agreement: I won't tell about you if you don't tell about me. In school, kids make faces behind the teacher's back and keep the knowledge as a group secret. The kid who tells is not well liked, especially if the telling is to curry favor with the teacher. Rivalry has its rules. This process of group loyalty helps a group pull together, to define its separate identity. However, a tension exists. Crimes and misdemeanors vary. A cookie snitched from the jar is not equivalent to a gun under the mattress. Some problems require intervention across generational or group boundaries. We frequently hear children, adolescents, and adults struggle with what is major and what is minor; what, when, and whom to tell. When do concerns about a larger good outweigh sibling or group loyalties? In professional groups—in all groups—collective unconscious sibling loyalty and conflicts over betrayal may undermine individual ego and superego functions, with defensive rationalizations and projections. Returning to the tragedy of Antigone, Ismene was caught in a loyalty conflict between the state and her sister.

Steve primarily chose patients as his love objects. Here Dr. Volkan's case contributes to our understanding of the role of sibling relationships in boundary violations. Dr. Volkan describes a man with a weak observing ego and a punitive superego, with projection and negation as primary defenses. He did not experience the people in his life as separate objects with their own motivations and feelings, precluding empathy for the effects of his actions on them. The capacity for an observing ego (or reflective function) and mature empathy rests on the development of mentalization. The capacity for mentalization is also necessary to develop the verbal symbolization surrounding thoughts, wishes, and feelings necessary to prevent an immediate discharge of drive-affect. (Lecours and Bouchard 1997). I would hypothesize that Steve had deficits in mentalization, and therefore was capable of empathy only as a toddler experiences it, which is as concordance or complementarity (Bolognini 1997). Thus, although he may have recognized feeling states in others, as does the toddler who soothes her crying mother, this function was based on primitive identifications. This is the constellation of a preoedipal morality, ego structure, and object relations. For Steve with his own patients, the subtly nuanced "as-if" nature of the psychotherapeutic experience would become "is." Because he lacks the superego and ego structures necessary for impulse control, his aggressive and sexual feelings for his mother and sister were actualized.

In a longer and unpublished report of this case, Volkan (1998, personal communication) speculated on Steve's moral masochism. Moral masochism is also discussed by Gabbard (1995) in his work on boundary violations. The moral masochist seeks punishment for unconscious incestuous and murderous fantasies, but not out of a fully developed sense of morality. What is sought is punishment, not reparation and change. Steve's superego was preoedipal, with the professional board and the analyst functioning as externalized superegos.

One can wonder about the aggressive nature of Steve's sexual transgressions with his patients, as well as the implicit aggression in having sex in front of his daughter. No matter how egalitarian a therapist tries to be, there is always a power differential in the relationship. Steve seems to have been drawn to relationships in which he would have power and the illusion of control. At the same time that Steve was having sex with the longed-for mother devoted exclusively to him, entering her womb, was he also omnipotently dominating and hurting the despised and potentially rejecting bad mother and siblings?

This brings us to the sexual aspects of Steve's involvements. Steve had sex with his patients, and also in front of his daughter. He was 6 when his sister was born. We can assume he had both dependent and genital sexual longings for his mother. What about his sister and his daughter? Sexual fantasies about siblings can be as charged as oedipal fantasies (Bank and Kahn 1982, Freud 1908). The instinctual danger may be powerful because of the lack of generational boundaries, the high access of siblings to one another, and the closeness in age and size (Agger 1997, Sharpe and Rosenblatt 1994). We know that these fantasies often lead to actual incest among siblings—heterosexual and homosexual—with potential deleterious impact on development (Bank and Kahn 1982). Additionally, when parents are emotionally unavailable, sexual fantasies toward siblings may become even more urgent, fueled by the need for libidinal supplies.

Steve's daughter was directly involved in the acting out of his conflicts. He called his daughter by his sister's name, and had sex in front of her. The story poignantly illustrates Selma Fraiberg's (Fraiberg et al. 1975) lasting and evocative concept of ghosts in the nursery. "Ghosts," as unresolved, rigid, and lasting endopsychic role representations, are projected from the parent onto the child. Steve's deficits in superego and ego structures necessary for impulse control and self observation enabled him to invoke his aggressive and sexual ghosts with his patients and his daughter. In this way, the unresolved and rigid sibling conflicts of one generation are recapitulated in the next (Sharpe and Rosenblatt 1994).

I think the words *unresolved* and *rigid* are key in describing these ghosts, because of course the inner worlds of all parents affect their children. In normal development the child assimilates and metabolizes a multitude of self- and object-derived introjections, projections, and projective identifications. The reflecting mirror of the parents' eyes gives back to the child an amalgamation of the child and the parents. The child's own constitutional, psychic, and somatic characteristics affect the way these early experiences with the minds of their parents and siblings are internalized. This process may actually help the child find a niche different from that of other siblings. However, when parental projections do not flexibly yield to the inner world of the child and to environmental realities, the process of individuation is undermined. The "niches" become jail cells rather than jumping-off points for individuation. Although it is not uncommon for people to revert to their assigned niches when reunited with siblings, as at family gatherings (Bank and Kahn 1982), one hopes that in the rest of life continued separation and individuation have provided flexible alternatives.

The concept of "ghosts in the nursery" is echoed in the findings of attachment theory. The attachment style of the child can be predicted by assessing, before the child's birth, the attachment style of the mother—not in all cases, but in the majority (Fonagy et al. 1995). Although to my knowledge the attachment theorists have not investigated sibling attachments, we can hypothesize from clinical psychoanalytic data that certain children may be especially vulnerable to these transferences because of birth order, gender, basic core, temperament, appearance, and other characteristics.

The Case of Lisa: A Womb Is Many Things

Dr. Volkan describes the unfolding of a "therapeutic story," in which Lisa's unconscious fantasies unfold in action outside the analytic room, but inside the analytic space. This case beautifully illustrates the many modes of communication between analyst and analysand, and reinforces the importance of listening and watching for derivatives of malignant and unresolved sibling rivalry. Lisa's womb fantasy, as it unfolded into consciously perceived analytic space, was of a particular kind—that of entering the womb, destroying the rival, and being the only occupant. This womb is a place of exclusive possession and bloody murder. Underlying this conception is her image of another kind of womb, in which "the walls were pink, soft and puffy, like cotton" (p. 132, this volume). There are many kinds of wombs, in metaphor and in derivatives, conscious and unconscious, with as many variations as there are people on the earth. The womb could represent merger, symbiosis, engulfment, a trap, retreat from separation and individuation, privacy, exclusive possession, sexual triumph, pregenital or genital erotic longings, timelessness, twinship, togetherness, primary female identification, reunion, eternal life, and so forth. The possessive and murderous womb is dramatic and may eclipse our awareness of other, quieter wombs, just as stories of murder and mayhem dominate the headlines.

Perhaps we cannot assume that "womb fantasies" exist per se. Rather they may be amalgamations of protosymbolic, psychosomatic, preverbal, and symbolic derivatives, emerging from all phases of life, and constantly reworked and reshaped through all phases of development. The form in which these fantasies then emerge in analysis would be structured by the analytic relationship, the person of the analyst and the analysand, the shared metaphors and symbols, and the nature of the transitional space between the two.

CONCLUSIONS: WOMB FANTASIES AND SIBLINGS IN PSYCHOANALYSIS

We certainly have much to learn by understanding how and why sibling rivalry runs amuck. Dr. Volkan clearly helps his analysands by being aware of sibling object relationships as important in their own right, and not just as representing displacements from the oedipal situation (Agger 1988, Bank and Kahn 1982, Graham 1988, Sharpe and Rosenblatt 1994). He discusses the relative neglect of sibling relationships in psychoanalytic thinking. We have to wonder why psychoanalysts, as aware as they are of the importance of early object relationships, have tended to focus on parents, with a relative neglect of siblings, or to regard conflicts around sibling relationships as a displacement from the parents. It is ironic that even in object relations and attachment theories, the role of siblings is minimized. Clearly this is multifaceted. Frued himself was an oldest sibling, favored by his mother, entitled within the family, and burdened by the death of a younger sibling occurring toward the end of his first year of life. His sister Anna, whom he disliked, was then born when he was about 2. Self analysis can go only so far. However, Freud himself has references to siblings. An example from "The Interpretation of Dreams" (1900) is: "Many people, therefore, who love their brothers and sisters, and would feel bereaved if they were to die, harbour evil wishes against them in their unconscious, dating from earlier times; and these are capable of being realized in dreams" (p. 203). The theoretical scotomata about siblings may lie with later psychoanalysts, as yet another example of how theory is shaped by intrapsychic and interpersonal conflict.

Intergenerational ghosts do not affect just families. They also haunt professional groups and disciplines. In psychoanalysis ancestral introjects and identifications are passed through training analyses and supervisions. Lacunae regarding siblings, and the defensive posture of minimizing or denying their influence, are perpetuated. After all, not acknowledging or talking about one's siblings is one way of getting rid of them. We frequently see this occurring in family life, when siblings isolate themselves with their own friends, ignore each other, or give the silent treatment. If not confronted and analyzed, this passive murder and denial will persist.

The very nature of the psychoanalytic situation may reinforce the tendency to minimize sibling issues or to reduce those issues to conflicts with parents. No matter how open and nonauthoritarian the analyst, the analytic encounter is asymmetric. Implicit power and authority differentials may favor, at least initially, the emergence of parental transferences. Using an example from another sphere, the gender of the analyst may influence the order in which the transferences emerge and evolve. At times patients are selectively referred to male or female analysts with the thought that immediate transferences may be specific to the analyst's gender. If, for example, the immediate paternal transferences may be so negative as to interfere with the development of a therapeutic alliance, that patient may do better with a female analyst. Eventually the negative paternal transferences will evolve, but after the formation of a solid working relationship.

Sibling transferences may be enacted outside the actual analysis. This may be with friends, colleagues, the actual siblings (Balsam 1998), or groups. Alternatively, sibling issues may emerge vis-à-vis fantasies (or the absence of fantasies) about other patients. Finally, in training analyses, other analysands are usually known to one another. It is very common for candidate analysands to refer to themselves as "analytic siblings." All these relationships may reflect intrapsychic sibling representations.

Child analysts may be especially aware of the importance of sibling relationships, at least for their child patients. Often the siblings are in the waiting room, frequently making noise or knocking at the door, and at times coming (invited or uninvited) into the treatment room. The child analyst may open her office door to call in the next child patient, to be granted by a screaming sibling fight and an overwhelmed parent. Parents often ask for guidance in handling sibling conflicts. The immediacy and power of sibling relationships in child analysis bring to mind a clinical vignette.

A 12-year-old girl with an eating disorder was beginning treatment with me. A colleague was to see the family for family therapy. The initial evaluation included a meeting with the parents, the patient, her 9-year-old sister, my colleague, and me. The mother sat on the couch with the two siblings on either side. My patient announced that she would readily participate in individual therapy, but wanted nothing to do with family therapy. I asked why. She stiffened, her usually neutral face tightened into a mask of disgust and rage, and she pointed her finger in the direction of her sister without looking at her. "Because of that!" she spat out. Her parents later emphasized that this was the first time they realized the extent of her rage and hatred.

REFERENCES

Abelin, E. (1971). The role of the father in the separation-individuation process. In *Separation-Individuation: Essays in Honor of Margaret Mahler*, ed. J. B. McDevitt and C. F. Settlage, pp. 229–252. New York: International Universities Press.

Agger, E. M. (1988). Psychoanalytic perspectives on sibling relationships. *Psychoanalytic Inquiry* 8:3–30.

―――― (1997). Sulloway and the imperatives of birth order. *Journal of the American Psychoanalytic Association* 45:1295–1301.

Balsam, R. H. (1988). On being good: the internalized sibling with examples from late adolescent analyses. *Psychoanalytic Inquiry* 8:66–87.

Bank, S. P., and Kahn, M. D. (1982). *The Sibling Bond*. Basic Books: New York.

Bolognini, S. (1997). Empathy and "empathism." *International Journal of Psycho-Analysis* 78:279-293.

Colonna, A. B., and Newman, L. M. (1983). The psychoanalytic literature on siblings. *Psychoanalytic Study of the Child* 38:285-308.

Fonagy, P., Steele, M., Steele, H., et al. (1995). The predictive specificity of the adult attachment interview and pathological emotional development. In *Attachment Theory: Social, Developmental, and Clinical Perspectives*, ed. S. Goldberg, R. Muir, and J. Kerr, pp. 233-278. Hillsdale NJ: Analytic Press.

Fraiberg, S., Adelson, E., and Shapiro V. (1975). Ghosts in the nursery: a psychoanalytic approach to the problems of impaired infant–mother relationships. *Journal of the American Academy of Child Psychiatry* 14:387-421.

Freud, A., and Dann, S. (1951). An experiment in group upbringing. *Psychoanalytic Study of the Child* 6:127-168. New York: International Universities Press.

Freud, S. (1900). The interpretation of dreams. *Standard Edition* 4:202-203.

—— (1908). On the sexual theories of children. *Standard Edition* 9:212:207-248.

—— (1909). Analysis of a phobia in a five year old boy. *Standard Edition* 10:3-149.

Gabbard, G. O. (1995). History of boundary violations. *Journal of the American Psychoanalytic Association* 43:1115-1136.

Graham, I. (1988). The sibling object and its transferences: alternate organizer of the middle field. *Psychoanalytic Inquiry* 8:88-107.

Hartmann, H. (1939). *Ego Psychology and the Problem of Adaptation*. New York: International Universities Press.

Kennell, J., Klaus, M., McGrath, S., et al. (1991). Continuous emotional support during labor in a US hospital. *Journal of the American Medical Association* 265:2197-2201.

Kernberg, P. A., and Richards, A. K. (1988). Siblings of preadolescents: their role in development. *Psychoanalytic Inquiry* 8:51-65.

Kestenberg, J. (1976). Regression and reintegration in pregnancy. *Journal of the American Psychoanalytic Association* 24:213-247.

Kris, M., and Ritvo, S. (1983). Parents and siblings—their mutual influence. *Psychoanalytic Study of the Child* 38:311-323. New Haven, CT: Yale University Press.

Lacan, J. (1959-1960). Book VII: The ethics of psychoanalysis. In *The Seminar of Jacques Lacan*, ed. J. A. Miller, pp. 243-287. New York: Norton, 1992.

Lecours, S., and Bouchard, M. A. (1997). Dimensions of mentalisation: outlining levels of psychic transformation. *International Journal of Psycho-Analysis* 78:855-875.

Leichtman, M. (1985). The influence of an older sibling on the separation-individuation process. *Psychoanalytic Study of the Child* 40:111-160. New Haven, CT: Yale University Press.

Mahler, M., Pine, F., and Bergman, A. (1975). *The Psychological Birth of the Human Infant*. New York: Basic Books.

Neubauer, P. B. (1982). Rivalry, envy, and jealousy. *Psychoanalytic Study of the Child* 37:121–141. New Haven, CT: Yale University Press.

—— (1983). The importance of the sibling experience. *Psychoanalytic Study of the Child* 38:325–336. New Haven, CT: Yale University Press.

Parens, H. (1988). Siblings in early childhood: some direct observational findings. *Psychoanalytic Inquiry* 8:31–50.

Provence, S., and Solnit, A. (1983). Development-promoting aspects of the sibling experience—vicarious mastery. *Psychoanalytic Study of the Child* 38:337–350.

Shakespeare, W. (1594). *The Tragedy of King Lear.* New York: Washington Square Press, 1993.

Shapiro, V., Fraiberg, S., and Adelson, E. (1976). Infant–parent psychotherapy on behalf of a child in a critical nutritional state. *Psychoanalytic Study of the Child* 31:461–491.

Sharpe, S. A., and Rosenblatt, A. D. (1994). Oedipal sibling triangles. *Journal of the American Psychoanalytic Association* 42:491–523.

Solnit, A. J. (1983). The sibling experience—introduction. *Psychoanalytic Study of the Child* 38:281–284.

Sophocles (442 BC, 435 BC, 446 BC). *Oedipus the King; Oedipus at Colonus; Antigone,* ed. D. Grene and R. Lattimore. New York: Washington Square Press, 1967.

Sulloway, F. (1996). *Born to Rebel: Birth Order, Family Dynamics, and Creative Lives.* New York: Pantheon.

Vestin, U. (1997). Antigone—a soul murder. *Psychoanalytic Quarterly* 66(1):82–92.

Webster's New World Dictionary of the American Language (1962). New York: World Publishing.

Winnicott, D. W. (1988). *Human Nature.* New York: Schocken.

8

BROTHERS AND SISTERS AND SIBLING RELATIONSHIPS

Concluding Reflections

Robert C. Prall, M.D.

"... and it came to pass, when they were in the field, that Cain rose up against Abel his brother, and slew him." Genesis 4:8 (King James version)

This year's 29th Annual Margaret S. Mahler Symposium on Child Development lives up to the reputation established over the years by Selma Kramer and her colleagues by delving into a subject that has been neglected by psychoanalysis to some extent until rather recently. The effect of siblings and their relationships and the impact of these on the development of intrapsychic self-representations and object representations of the siblings within each others' psyches was explored from three contrasting points of view. All of the papers focused on the fundamental postulates of our mentor, Margaret Mahler, who, I feel sure, would have been pleased with these contributions to the understanding of child development and the application of her concepts in the psychoanalytic treatment of adults.

First, Ricardo Ainslie drew upon his extensive experience in the study of twins to present a most valuable and lucid paper on the subject of "Twinship and Twinning Reactions in Siblings." The discussion of this paper by Henri Parens showed his depth of understanding of child development, and, in particular, twin and sibling relationships, and complemented Dr. Ainslie's coverage of this subject.

Second, Rosemary Balsam presented an unusual discussion of "Sisters and Their Disappointing Brothers" in a paper about the inner world of female gender development in powerful women with brothers who presented unusual problems in the family setting during their childhoods. These families were in marked contrast to those more frequently encountered in the psychoanalytic literature in which the son is favored and the daughter is denigrated.

Third, Vamık Volkan's paper on "Childhood Sibling Rivalry and Unconscious Womb Fantasies in Adults" dealt with his understanding of the unconscious fantasies of adult patients, referring in particular to unconscious womb fantasies as they were uncovered in adult analytic work. All of the adult patients described were eldest children whose siblings were born in the first six years of their lives. The births of these siblings had a profound effect on their psychic development.

A brilliant discussion of Volkan's paper by Barbara Shapiro included the relevant literary antecedents of the legend of Oedipus, his two sons and two daughters, and their tragic ends, as depicted by Sophocles. She pointed out that "malignant sibling hatred and destructive repetitions of the past do not spring up in a vacuum" (this volume, p. 140).

HISTORICAL PERSPECTIVE

Sibling relationships, rivalry, and jealousy are as old as recorded history. The Old Testament is replete with evidence of great rivalry and hatred between brothers and to some extent between sisters. The custom of primogeniture, giving the first-born the father's blessings and his inheritance, was the cause of much strife.

For example, Isaac's wife, Rebekah, had twin sons, Esau and Jacob. "And the children struggled together within her; . . . And the Lord said unto her, two nations are in thy womb . . . and the one people shall be stronger than the other people; and the elder shall serve the younger" (Genesis 25:22–23). (Interestingly, Parens, in his discussion of Ainslie's paper, refers to the possibility of twins' recognition of each other's presence in intrauterine life. Ainslie reported in his twin studies that later in life one twin would accuse the other of kicking him out of the womb or of pressing on his umbilical cord in utero in the belief that this accounted for his smaller size.)

When the elder son, Esau, was starving, Jacob gave him food in exchange for his birthright (Genesis 25:34). Rebekah preferred Jacob and when Isaac was old and blind she conspired to help Jacob get his father's blessing away from Esau. Isaac had told Esau, the hunter, to go kill an animal for him to eat and that he would bless him before he died. But Rebekah cooked some meat and put Esau's raiment on Jacob and goat skins on his hands and neck to fool the blind Isaac into thinking that smooth-skinned Jacob was really hairy Esau, and Isaac blessed Jacob instead of Esau.

When Esau heard this he cried bitterly—" . . . and Esau hated Jacob because of the blessing . . . and Esau said in his heart . . . then will I slay my brother Jacob" (Genesis 27:41).

Many years later, Jacob, fearing that his brother would come and kill him, sent Esau a present of livestock of great value and the brothers were reunited. (Jacob also brought a full army with him to the reunion, not knowing how Esau would receive him and his gifts.) "And Esau ran to meet him, and embraced him, and fell on his neck and kissed him: and they wept" (Genesis 33:4).

Among other biblical references to sibling rivalry and hatred is the story of Joseph, who at 17 was hated by his brothers because Jacob loved Joseph more than all his other children and made him a coat of many colors. "And when his brethren saw that their father loved him more than all his brethren, they hated him . . . they conspired against him to slay him" (Genesis 37:4, 18).

After his brothers threw him into a pit and stained his coat with blood, he was sold into slavery and he ended up in Egypt where he became the Pharaoh's favorite when he predicted the seven years of plenty and seven years of famine from Pharaoh's dreams. When famine struck, his brothers came to Egypt from Canaan to buy food from him, and after some machinations, Joseph revealed himself and forgave his brothers for their treachery.

Thus, we see in these episodes of fierce sibling rivalry and hatred that ambivalence and good feelings between the siblings were also present.

Another fascinating Biblical story tells of the twins Pharez and Zarah being born to Tamar, the widow of Er. When Zarah reached out his arm first, the midwife bound a scarlet thread upon his hand, saying, "this came out first." However, he retracted his arm and Pharez was born first, which surely must have been to the consternation of all concerned as the midwife said, "How hast thou broken forth? This breach be upon thee" (Genesis 38:28–29).

Rivalry and jealousy were not limited to male children in the Bible. The sisters Rachel and Leah were also envious of each other. Jacob loved Rachel and had worked for her father, Laban, for seven years to earn the right to marry her. However, Laban switched daughters and had Leah lie with him instead, saying that it was not proper for the younger to marry before the firstborn. Jacob worked for another seven years to be able also to marry Rachel. The rivalry between Leah and Rachel was quite heated. When Rachel bore no children, she envied her sister who had children, and Leah protested that Rachel had stolen her husband.

Perhaps the most far-reaching sibling rivalry and strife in the Old Testament is the story of the births of Abram's (Abraham's) two sons, Ishmael and Isaac. Sarai (Sarah), Abram's wife, was barren. The Lord had promised Abram a long line of descendants, so Sarai gave her Egyptian handmaid, Hagar, to Abram to be his concubine. "And Hagar bare Abram a son: and Abram called his son's name, which Hagar bare, Ishmael" (Genesis 16:15).

When Abram was 100 years old, God worked a miracle. "For Sarah conceived and bare Abraham a son in his old age . . . and Abraham called . . . him Isaac" (Genesis 21:2-3). Sarah told Abraham to cast out the bondwoman and her son. Abraham was grieved but sent them away. God said to Abraham, "And also the son of the bondwoman will I make a nation, because he is thy seed" (Genesis 21:13).

Thus, the two nations, Islam and the Judeo-Christian world, were separated and have remained at swords' points until the present day, as evidenced, for example, by the continuous strife between the Israelis and the Palestinians.

Having just returned from Dr. Vamık's home country, Cyprus, three days before the Mahler Symposium, I was made aware of the tremendous tensions and strife between the world of Islam and the Judeo-Christian world. Cyprus is a divided island. The Islamic Turkish northern part is walled off by the "green line," manned by United Nations troops, from the Greek Orthodox southern portion of the island. Since the Turkish invasion in 1974, great tension and suspicion, originating many centuries ago, continues to exist between these two ethnic groups as so clearly described by Volkan (1979) in his book, *Cyprus—War and Adaptation*.

Strife and wars between the Islamic and Judeo-Christian factions have been highlighted by the three Crusades with their slaying of "the infidels," Saladin's defeating the Crusaders in

Syria, the Turkish invasion of Cyprus, and the attacks on Malta in attempts to drive out the Knights of St. John of Jerusalem. Malta never fell but the Turks captured the Maltese island of Gozo and enslaved the entire population of thousands. The expansion of the Ottoman Empire was finally stopped but there is still constant strife between such neighbors as Turkey and Greece; Israel, Egypt, Syria, Lebanon, and Jordan, to name but a few instances of the ongoing conflict. It becomes obvious that the results of sibling rivalries and hatred may also be seen on an international scale. Rivalry between "brothers" can extend to enduring conflicts between ethnic groups such as in Bosnia, Croatia, and now Kosovo.

MYTHOLOGY

Roman mythology also gives evidence of rivalrous sibling situations. In one myth, twins were born to a beautiful princess who had been imprisoned by her uncle, a usurper. She became pregnant, ostensibly by the god Mars, and gave birth to the twins, Romulus and Remus. The uncle sent them to be abandoned in the open country so that they would be devoured by wild animals. However, as with Oedipus, fate intervened and they were placed in a basket that floated down the Tiber to the Palatine where a she-wolf nursed them until a shepherd found them and took them home to his wife to nurture and raise. The myth states that when they were grown they displaced the usurper. Romulus killed Remus and founded Rome in 753 BC.

In Greek mythology, the story of Castor and Pollux, the twin sons of Leda by Zeus disguised as a swan, is complicated by another myth that Leda also slept with her husband, Tyndareus, that same night and she bore two sets of twins. In one egg were Castor and Clytemnestra while in the other were Pollux and Helen. As young men, Castor and Pollux abducted the brides-to-be of their cousins, Idas and Lynceus. As a result, Idas killed Castor and Pollux slew Lynceus. Eventually, Castor and Pollux became the constellation Gemini, the twins.

These myths indicate the extent of sibling rivalry and jealousy throughout the ages.

Of course, there is the other side of the coin, the ambivalently loved sibling. History and mythology tell us of many incestuous relationships between siblings.

The fairy tale of "Hansel and Gretel" gives evidence of a close, affectionate, protective relationship between two siblings. The children are living in a poverty-stricken home with little to eat and are sent out into the forest to gather strawberries by the wicked stepmother, who hopes that they will be eaten by wild animals. They become lost and wander in the forest until dark when they huddle together for protection and fall asleep in each other's arms. In the morning they discover the witch's gingerbread house and begin to eat. The witch entraps them and plans to eat them as she had many other children, but Hansel and Gretel outwit the witch (bad mother) and push her into the oven. The father finds them and they are happily reunited.

CHILD ANALYSIS

Our child analytic work reveals much evidence of the ambivalence between siblings that casts its shadow throughout peoples' lifetimes and affects their object choices, choices of mates, relationships with their children, and their aversions to others, much of which is often noted in the transference.

As a child analyst working with many children, I see daily the impact of the birth of a new sibling on the psychic development of children. Child analysts, who are so familiar with the sibling struggles in their child patients, are more likely to be tuned in to the impact of sibling relationships with their adult patients.

Case 1

Walt, who is 4 years old, has a younger brother age 16 months and a baby sister born two weeks ago. With this young child, I am able to see the development in *status nascendi* of a myriad of womb fantasies reminiscent of Volkan's paper at this symposium as well as his recent co-authored book, *Siblings in the Unconscious and Psychopathology* (Volkan and Ast 1997).

Walt's most striking recent play has centered upon his making my "Big Bird" puppet the mother. He has repeatedly placed my two stone eggs, one alabaster and the other onyx, into Big Bird's "tummy" and had her deliver the babies. He then placed all kinds of figures in the puppet and repeatedly had her deliver them. Walt often spoke of his mother's tummy being big and fat before the baby was born and he showed this in his play by stuffing more and more objects into the "mother's" (Big Bird's) tummy. This play was accompanied by much oral and anal aggression. He took my toy fish and had it eat everything in sight and then had it make "poo-poo" all over everything. The sharks' teeth in my shell collection fascinated him and he had them devour many baby figures and the eggs as well. Finally, holding his nose, he said, "The baby cries too much and makes poopy dipes. Pee-uuu!"

At the next visit, Walt found a mother panda puppet that has twin babies in a pouch in her bottom. This discovery resulted in much birth play and return to the womb, first by one baby and then the other, and sometimes both of them together. There was evidence of much rivalry between the twin babies for the mother's attention and to see who could get back into the womb first. Again, simultaneously, oral and anal aggression were paramount in the play. He then began to grab his penis over and over and finally retreated to the bathroom to urinate. Then he resumed the birth and rebirth fantasy play.

From reconstruction with adult patients Volkan postulated that, at the birth of a younger sibling, many patients develop womb fantasies of wishing to climb back into the mother's womb to kill the baby intruder. It will be interesting to follow further the development of Walt's fantasies about the birth of his younger siblings to see what develops next.

TWINS

Ainslie's presentation on twinship and twinning reactions shows the depth of his understanding of twins derived from his many years of study of twinships (Ainslie 1985, 1997). He reviews the psychoanalytic literature on the influence of siblings in child development, pointing out that the earlier assumption in analytic thinking that siblings represent a displacement from the parent of the same sex is giving way to a more precise awareness of the meaning of siblings in psychic development. "In sum, the proposition that siblings play a more substantive role in development than previously theorized is increasingly, if cautiously, explored in the psychoanalytic literature" (this volume, p. 29).

He explores the concept of twinning reactions as consisting of "(1) mutual interidentification, and (2) part fusion of the self-representation and the object representation of the other member of the pair" (this volume, p. 29). Twinning reactions may be accompanied by polarization of various traits in the twin pair, such as male/female, passive/active, stronger/weaker, in an effort to circumvent rivalry and competition. This may also be influenced by parental fantasies about their children and by identifications with the parents. Failure to establish adequate self–object differentiation, and regressive blurring of boundaries between the twins lead to twins referring to themselves as "we" rather than "I."

Ainslie clearly discusses difficulties experienced by twins in the various stages of the separation-individuation process, in par-

ticular, symbiosis and rapprochement. He highlights the stress
often experienced by parents in meeting the needs of twins simultaneously and the fatigue so often experienced by the over-
burdened parents. An interesting point that he makes is that
twins may use each other as quasi-transitional objects. However,
one twin does not have total control over the other as one has
with a true transitional object (Winnicott 1953).

Throughout Dr. Ainslie's presentation, I was often reminded of my own analytic work with an identical twin. Defects in self-representation and twinning reactions were prominent features for this girl. She often stated that she felt like half
a person when her twin sister was not with her and she constantly referred to herself as "we."

Case 2

Mizzy, an 11-year-old identical twin who has been described
elsewhere (Prall 1990), was first seen in a hospital bed
where she was close to death from anorexia, having lost
half of her body weight. In the analysis that was begun immediately it soon became apparent that, as she approached
puberty, she had begun to exercise furiously and had
stopped eating and was starving herself to keep from developing "a front" (breasts) like her older sisters and
mother.

The background included the fact that the father did
not want any more children since there were already two
older sisters, Sophie and Sarah, in the family. He said that
at least he didn't want any more girls. When the twin girls
were born, Lizzy became mother's girl and Mizzy, father's
girl.

The parents used nail polish on the twins in order to
tell them apart. As infants they slept together, sucked each
other's thumbs and masturbated each other, which con-
firms Ainslie's observations about twins using each other

for soothing and stimulation when the external supplies are insufficient.

As they grew into latency on the farm where they lived, Mizzy became her father's companion and helper. She adopted a boy's name, assisted her father with carpentry work, and helped him castrate the lambs and dock their tails. Lizzy was the more feminine twin who dressed up and tried to act like a lady.

The twins obviously developed different personality traits that divided up into male/female, industrious/lazy, superego/id, active/passive. Mizzy did all of the work, such as mucking out the horse stables, while Lizzy sat around reading comic books. Mizzy set the table and helped their mother with meals while Lizzy did little to help. Mizzy did the homework for both of them and would sneak into Lizzy's classroom to take her place when Lizzy wasn't prepared for a school assignment.

In an unconscious attempt to maintain her male identity and male self-representation, Mizzy had attempted, by the psychologically determined anorexia, to delay her puberty development. Lizzy began to menstruate a full year before Mizzy, a manifestation of the power of psychological forces over physiological processes.

One of the striking fantasies that emerged in the analysis was that Mizzy had a fantasy triplet who was perfect, never fought or argued, and never got into trouble. This triplet seemed to represent a projection and externalization of Mizzy's ego ideal as it behaved the way she aspired to behave.

When I discussed this fantasy with Anna Freud and Dorothy Burlingham (personal communication, 1968), they indicated that they had never encountered such triplet fantasies in their work with twins. Of course, we are all familiar with the twin fantasies of single children (Burlingham 1945) but this triplet fantasy seems to be a rather unusual occurrence.

Mizzy had great difficulty working through the separation-individuation process. As "father's girl," she had received less close attention from her mother as a baby than had Lizzy and, consequently, her symbiotic attachment to their mother was less satisfactory than that of her sister, who was "mother's girl." In addition, her symbiotic attachment of Lizzy was very powerful as the twins had turned to each other for sustenance. The working through of her separation-individuation from Lizzy was a time-consuming task in the analysis.

SISTERS WITH DEFECTIVE BROTHERS

In Dr. Rosemary Balsam's chapter, "Sisters and Their Disappointing Brothers," she describes two families in which the daughters were successful, talented, and competitive career women. They were both favored and their brothers were each denigrated. Balsam rejects the patriarchal and phallocentric viewpoint and focuses on women's attributes rather than on their lacks.

Patient A.'s younger brother was severely disabled with childhood autism and caused great tension and screaming in the home, culminating in the parents' divorce. As a child she had tortured him and played with his penis and threatened to cut it off if he told their parents. In adolescence, she became close to her father, who took her on trips and indulged her, and she developed a powerful adolescent oedipal bond.

Patient B. was 3 years old when her older brother, who was severely handicapped from spina bifida, died at the age of 5. The wealthy parents of this defective son must have been greatly distressed and depressed at giving birth to a severely damaged child. After his death, their attention turned to the sister, who became the focus of all their hopes and aspirations.

She had become a successful business woman and the heir apparent to the family's fortune.

In both of these families Balsam notes that the girls were grossly favored and held all the hopes of the family. They became highly ambitious, competitive, and successful in their careers and had durable self-esteem but had difficulties in their intimate relationships with men.

This presentation reminded me of two recent novels by Barbara Taylor Bradford, *A Woman of Substance* (1979) and *Hold That Dream* (1985). These novels are about the powerful women in the clan of Emma Harte, who was able to rise from poverty and disgrace after she was taken into the Fairley household as a servant where she was raped and impregnated by one of the men in the family and then discarded by them. Emma was able to use her ego strength to amass great wealth and she managed to take over all the Fairley family holdings and many more properties and become a veritable tycoon.

There was tremendous sibling rivalry among her children, including the one born of the rape and those from various marriages who were jealous of each other and who strove to acquire Emma's wealth by insidious means. In the second novel, Emma's granddaughter, Emily, having been carefully nurtured and tutored by her grandmother, carries on Emma's tradition of besting powerful men in their boardrooms, where women had not appeared before, as she contined to amass even greater fortunes.

In the discussion of the chapters by Drs. Ainslie and Balsam, Dr. Volkan pointed out that not all twins develop psychopathology. He likened twinning reactions to imaginary companions, where a child projects part of himself and some internal object representations as well as ego functions onto the imaginary companion, who is under the absolute control of the child. He indicated that when the twins are of different sexes there is often much struggle with body image formation. The twins may seem at times to function like a three-legged team similar to those seen in sack races in which children are paired each with one leg in a sack.

Dr. Blum discussed Ainslie's twin paper and indicated that even with identical twins, the twins are never completely identical. There are differences in birth weight and in mitochondria and DNA. He added that the trajectory of twinning reactions begins in the womb between the "wombmates" who share a common space and who encroach upon each other. The viscissitudes of uneven birth weight, birth complications, and differences in intrauterine development affect the twins' early maturation and may validate in one way or another the mother's prebirth fantasies about the twins.

CHILDHOOD SIBLING EXPERIENCES AND WOMB FANTASIES IN ADULTS

In the afternoon session, Dr. Volkan's presentation focused on analytic work with adults, all of whom had had younger siblings born during the first six years of their lives. His paper focused on the womb fantasies displayed by these patients. The older sibling wished to climb back into the womb and kill the intruder who threatened his relationship with the mother. A second fantasy was of the patient climbing back into the womb and encountering the father's penis, a one-eyed Cyclops, along with the unborn baby.

Volkan described the treatment of a 16-year-old boy who perceived the birth of his younger sister as a catastrophe and unconsciously turned his aggression toward her onto himself. He attempted to disappear by a suicide attempt and by running away and also seemed to try to disappear in his oversized clothing. A second case was that of a mental health professional whose unconscious sibling experiences were remobilized at the time of the birth of his daughter, whom he perceived as the incarnation of the mental representation of his younger sister.

He suffered from depression and intermittent suicidal thoughts. The therapist felt that an infantile trauma at the birth of the sister was reactivated by the birth of his own children and that the mental representations of the original objects were recathected. His murderous wishes toward his younger siblings, who he felt were responsible for the loss of his mother, were displaced onto his own children and kept him in constant fear for their safety. As treatment progressed, he began to call his daughter by his sister's name, confirming the unconscious association of the two girls. His extraordinary need for attention and affection from women led him to become involved with a series of his women patients, resulting in an investigation of his professional behavior. From these and his other patients, Volkan postulated that the birth of younger siblings led to womb fantasies that became unconscious and were connected with the patient's psychopathology.

In her fascinating discussion of Volkan's paper, Dr. Barbara Shapiro turned to the Oedipus myth to discuss the fierce sibling rivalry between the sons of Oedipus and also between his daughters. In the end all four met tragic deaths. She spoke of the relationships between older siblings and their younger intruders, along with the younger child's coming to actively compete with the older for things and for the parents' attention. The younger sibling's rivalry is often mixed with adoration and imitation. Shapiro discussed four contributing factors that may keep sibling rivalry from becoming structured into malignant hatred: (1) the adequacy of maternal libidinal supplies, (2) the parents' maintaining their love for all of the children, (3) a continuing positive relationship between the parents and supportive relationships for the mother, and (4) the attachment of the baby for the older sibling. Shapiro pointed out that even the most optimum conditions cannot prevent rivalry based on emotions that are part of our everyday lives when we live in proximity to others. She explained the derivation of the word *rivalry* from the Latin *rivalis*, meaning "one living near or using the same stream as another." She continued, "We can learn mutual cooperation, coordination, and sharing—major ego functions—so that everyone has access to clean water. Alternatively we can pollute the water, block access, or engage in open warfare. Obviously, if the water supply is inadequate or already contaminated, rivalry becomes a fight for either one or the other to survive" (this volume, p. 146). In her discussion of Dr. Volkan's cases, Shapiro commented on the unconscious womb fantasies he described and pointed out that there can be many other kinds of womb fantasies. She stated, "The womb could represent merger, symbiosis, engulfment, a trap, retreat from separation and individuation, privacy, exclusive possession, sexual triumph, pregenital or genital erotic longings, timelessness, twinship, togetherness, primary female identification, reunion, eternal life, and so forth" (this volume, p. 153).

Shapiro concludes by indicating that the form in which womb fantasies may "emerge in analysis would be structured by the analytic relationship, the person of the analyst and the analysand, . . . and the nature of the transitional space between the two" (this volume, p. 154).

DISCUSSION

In the general discussion, many points were emphasized by the panel and members of the audience. In his response to Dr. Shapiro's discussion, Volkan agreed that there are various types of womb fantasies and that not all of them are negative and hostile. He pointed out that there is an unconscious transgenerational transmission from the mother (parents) to the child of the mother's shortcomings and of cultural issues. The mother's fantasies and mental representations of the baby are unconsciously transmitted to the child and have a powerful effect on the child's psychic development.

At the Center for the Study of Mind and Human Interaction at the University of Virginia, Volkan and his colleagues

are studying world issues and the unconscious mental representations of shared trauma that are transmitted to the next generation, thus prolonging interethnic strife. He gave an illustration of transmission of a mother's fantasies to her child. This
mother thought her child was a beautiful baby but was concerned that the child might bite off her own fingers. The maternal grandmother told the mother that as a child she was such
a nice sister, except that one day she had found her with her
new baby brother's fingers in her mouth and had said, "What
are you doing?! You bit the baby's fingers." The mother had
protested, "I'm tasting him!" When she showed such anxiety
about her daughter biting off her own fingers, we see evidence
of the mother's unfinished business in her unconscious fantasies becoming transmitted to her daughter.

Volkan stated that with transsexuals, the mother's unconscious representations of the baby are transmitted to the child
and have a powerful impact on the child's gender identity formation.

Dr. Balsam questioned Dr. Volkan about these types of
womb fantasies as to whether the analyst found only what he
was looking for. Dr. Volkan answered that he did not find these
types of womb fantasies in younger siblings, but only in older
siblings and added that one finds many other types of womb
fantasies as well.

Selma Kramer spoke of a case of transgenerational transmission of unconscious fantasies with a little boy whom she had
treated. The mother felt that her son looked like her Uncle
Louie who was an undesirable person and was in jail. Her expectations for her son were that he would turn out to be just
like Uncle Louie and would also end up in jail. She was unable
to tolerate or nurture the child. Dr. Kramer referred the mother
for treatment before beginning therapy with the little boy.

Dr. Kramer also told of an adult male patient who had had
very poor fathering, whereas his sister had had marvelous fathering. When his sister was pregnant with her second child,

this man freely talked about his fantasies that the baby would burst out through a hole in her uterus and abdomen and the baby would bleed to death and so would she. Kramer pointed out that it is not just the mother who determines the child's psychic development but also the father. Men who have had poor fathering suffer from serious psychological consequences as well.

In the discussion, I pointed out that, in contrast to the emphasis on the negative aspects of sibling rivalry and jealousy in today's presentations, there are often many delightful and positive experiences in the relationships among siblings. From close observations of my own five children and now my grandchildren, I have seen great joy, love, pride, and pleasure expressed by an older sibling holding the baby tenderly with a broad grin and saying such things as, "She's my baby!" The older sibling has often been very helpful to the mother in caring for and feeding the baby.

The possibilities of pleasurable and joyful sibling experiences are in direct proportion to the child's positive self-image and, in turn, the quality of the libidinal availability of the mothering that she herself has enjoyed. Her pleasure in taking care of the baby is by way of a positive identification with a loving, "good enough" mother (Winnicott 1958).

When there are less than optimal libidinal supplies available or there is overt hostility toward or rejection of the older child, the result will be problematic sibling relationships and intense sibling jealousy, rivalry, and hatred.

Parens agreed with this point of view and added that there is a positive side to sibling relationships and that having a newborn sibling is an average expectable event. Single children show the absence of having the experience of siblings, for example, in having no one with whom to struggle and with whom to learn to share.

Even in the colleagues' discussions of each other's papers, we see some evidence of sibling relationship problems. Harold

Blum elaborated on the extension of womb fantasies beyond the murderous dual destructiveness aspects that were discussed in this Symposium. In addition, he pointed out that the womb may represent many things, including symbiosis and merger. Blum said that womb fantasies first turned up in psychoanalytic thinking in the "oceanic feeling" discussed between Freud and the renowned author Romain Rolland (see Jones 1957 and Freud 1930). The fear and wish for reunion and return to the womb in life's trajectory from womb to tomb may be manifested by death anxiety, which may be related to the equivalence of "womb/tomb" fantasies. The anxiety may reflect unconscious fantasies of reunion such as the "oceanic" feeling of reunion, the feeling of "oneness with the universe," which may represent a return to "mother earth." The religious "oceanic" experience may have a negative side as, for example, with Virginia Woolf, who walked into the water to drown herself—a symbolic reunion with the water (womb/mother).

Blum also spoke of Leonardo da Vinci and the Mona Lisa, which was painted over a period of four years. He kept the model with him and he would not part with the painting. He took the Mona Lisa with him wherever he went. Her smile represented the smile of the incompletely separated lost biological mother. He was invited to Paris where he died with the Mona Lisa.

Dr. Bert Ruttenberg asked about the advisability of keeping twins together in school versus separating them. Dr. Ainslie responded that there is no axiomatic reason to separate twins. If they are engaged in developmental tasks appropriate for their age there is no obvious reason to separate them. The close relationship with each other and the quality of their object relationships must be taken into account. We must look at each twinship individually to determine the best way to proceed.

Ainslie also pointed out that twins tend to arouse a feeling of envy in others since all kinds of wishful fantasies can be projected upon them. The film *Dead Ringer* depicts the existence

of such envy quite well. Also, whether twins should be kept
together or separated from each other is a decision that almost
invariably gets caught up in and colored by the projection of
the observer's own unconscious issues regarding attachment and
separation. Ainslie described a humorous episode in one family he had studied with a mother pregnant with twins who had
a 5-year-old son who shared the bed with his parents. This
mother said that they will now have to change their customs
since there won't be room for five people in the bed.

Dr. Parens agreed with Dr. Ainslie about the issue of separating twins and indicated that in our work we can help twins
differentiate from the mother and each other.

Rosemary Balsam added that sometimes mothers of twins
are confused in their intrapsychic representations of the twins.
One mother was distressed that she could not tell which twin
was which in a photograph. Another mother told Dr. Ainslie
of having nursed one of her twins and that she was upset because she thought that she was nursing the other one.

If I may give a personal example, my 2-year-old brother
died of influenza when I was 4 years old. We had been quite
close and I was very attached to him. The family photograph
album shows ample evidence of our attachment. For example,
in one picture in the snow I am holding my little brother pro-
tectively on my lap on a sled while our older brother is stand-
ing behind us holding a giant snowball over us, about to crash
it upon our heads. We were allied as a pair, defending against
our more aggressive older brother who had had to endure the
births of *two* younger siblings, which doubtless stirred up much
hostility and envy on his part which, incidentally, still exists to
this day in his old age.

However, in spite of my conscious memories of my fond-
ness for "Baby John," in my analysis unconscious fantasies and
death wishes toward my little brother were uncovered. One dramatic revelation came in a dream in which I was trying to throw
him off a roof.

My affection for him, plus reaction formation and sublimation of my aggression toward him, may account, in part, for why I became a child analyst to try to help other children with their difficulties. It also may help explain why I enjoy children so much, especially why I get such pleasure from watching the development of my grandchildren and great grandchildren. Unfortunately, my older brother is unable to enjoy either his children or his grandchildren at least in part due to unresolved unconscious childhood rivalry and hostility toward his younger brothers whose intrapsychic representations are projected and displaced onto his own offspring.

REFERENCES

Ainslie R. C. (1985). *The Psychology of Twinship.* Lincoln, NE: University of Nebraska Press.

—— (1997). *The Psychology of Twinship.* Northvale, NJ: Jason Aronson.

Bradford, B. T. (1979). *A Woman of Substance.* New York: Avon.

—— (1985). *Hold That Dream.* New York: Bantam.

Burlingham, D. T. (1945). The fantasy of having a twin. *Psychoanalytic Study of the Child* 1:205–210. New York: International Universities Press.

Freud, S. (1930). Civilization and its discontents. *Standard Edition* 21:59–145.

Jones, E. (1957). *The Life and Work of Sigmund Freud,* vol. 3. New York: Basic Books.

Prall, R. C. (1990). The neurotic adolescent. In *The Neurotic Child and Adolescent,* ed. M. H. Etezady, pp. 241–302. Northvale, NJ: Jason Aronson.

Volkan, V. D. (1979). *Cyprus—War and Adaptation: A Psychoanalytic History of Two Ethnic Groups in Conflict.* Charlottesville, VA: University Press of Virginia.

Volkan, V. D., and Ast, G. (1997). *Siblings in the Unconscious and Psychopathology.* Madison, CT: International Universities Press.

Winnicott, D. W. (1953). Transitional objects and phenomena. *International Journal of Psycho-Analysis* 34:89–97.

—— (1958). *Collected Papers.* New York: Basic Books.

Index